# ANXIETY

## The Way In. The Way Out.

Simon Robinson

ANXIETY: THE WAY IN. THE WAY OUT.



This edition is a substantially revised and expanded work,
distinct in structure, content, and presentation from earlier editions
previously published under the same title.

Revised edition published 2025

ISBN (Paperback): 978-1-0684310-9-8

Simon Robinson
www.drsimonrobinson.com

Printed and distributed by IngramSpark
Printed in Australia, UK and USA

READER NOTICE:

This book reflects personal experience and interpretation.
It is not medical advice and does not replace professional care.

If you are feeling unsafe, overwhelmed, or at risk of harming yourself, please seek immediate support from a healthcare professional or a trusted local crisis service.

*This book does not ask you to move faster than you can.*

*Nothing here requires agreement, belief, or endurance.*

*If at any point the material feels like too much,*

*stopping is part of the work.*

# Chapter 1

*Fear is already here.*
*It arrives without invitation, without explanation.*
*I notice it before I know what it is for, as if it belongs to the body more than to thought.*

*My body reacts faster than my mind can follow.*
*Something tightens, even though nothing is happening.*
*The signal feels urgent, but its origin remains unclear.*

*I notice how rarely I feel safe.*
*Not unsafe—just without safety.*
*The absence has become ordinary.*

*Heat moves through me.*
*Pressure gathers and releases.*
*My body acts before I can follow it.*

*Sometimes there is no movement at all.*
*Everything pauses.*
*I disappear into the stillness.*

*The moment passes.*
*Then it returns.*
*Each time, it feels immediate again.*

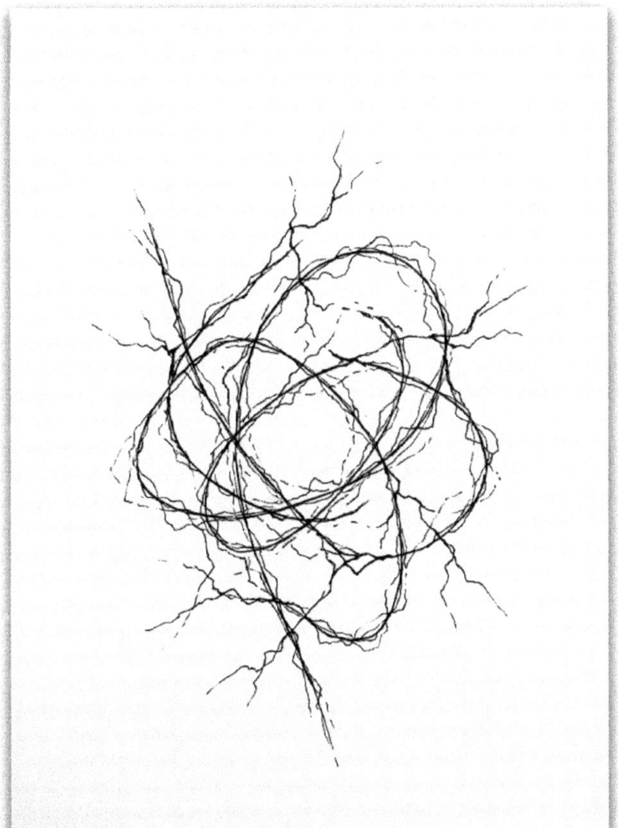

*I notice myself watching.*

*Even rest feels exposed.*

*Attention does not know where to land.*

*This feeling is old.*
*It learned me before I could name it.*
*The body remembers first.*

*I begin to doubt the feeling itself.*
*I wonder if it is telling the truth.*
*The question creates a little space.*

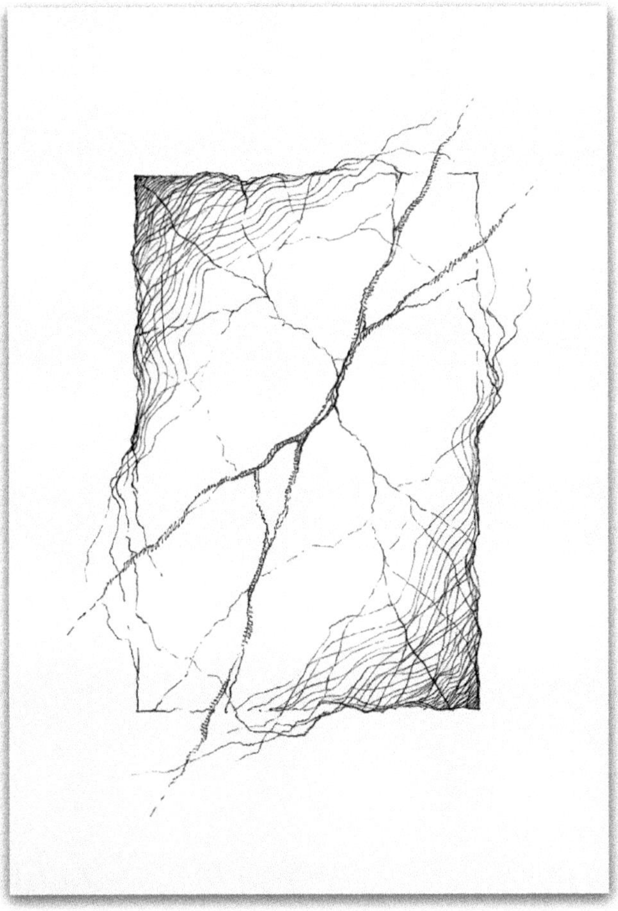

*I imagine fear happening over there.*
*Here, there is room.*
*I stay with what remains.*

*There is a place that can hold what I cannot.*
*I do not enter it.*
*It remains closed, and that is enough.*

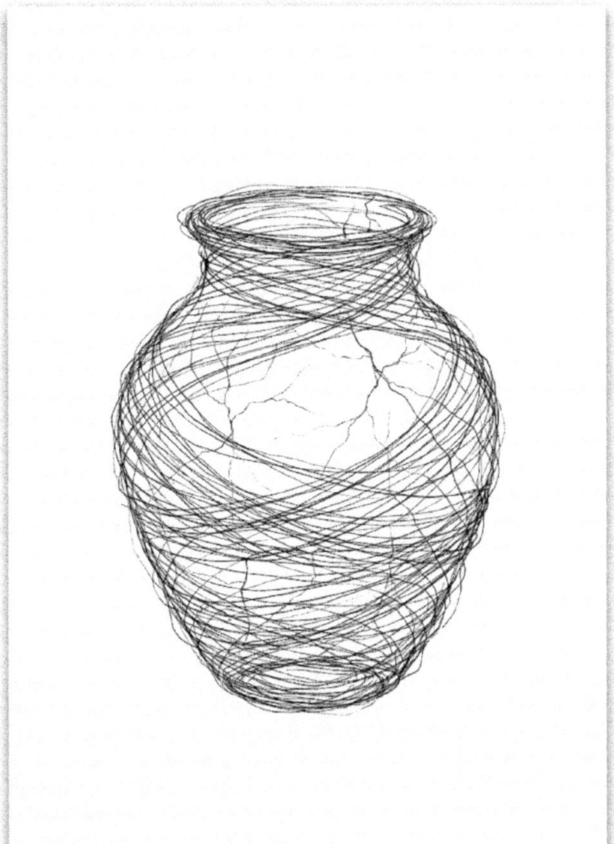

*Something moves on without me watching.*
*Time passes.*
*I am not required to follow it.*

*Nothing is solved.*
*But there is space now.*
*I remain here.*

# Chapter 2

*My system turns on before I decide anything.*
*There is a familiar pull in three directions.*
*I recognise it without choosing it.*

*The moment ends, but something keeps going.*
*A low hum remains, without a source.*
*Time does not reset cleanly.*

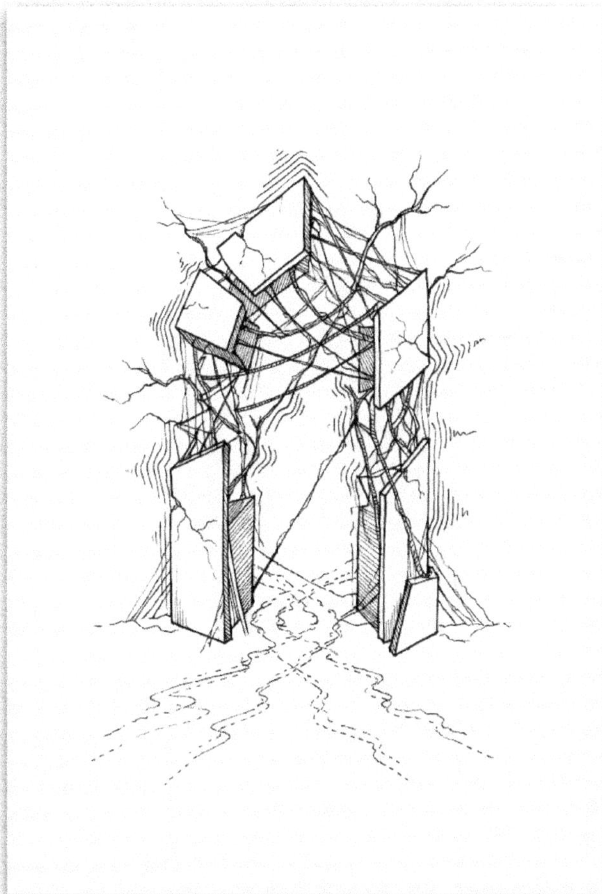

*I become watchful by habit.*
*Attention keeps scanning.*
*Nothing appears, but the scanning continues.*

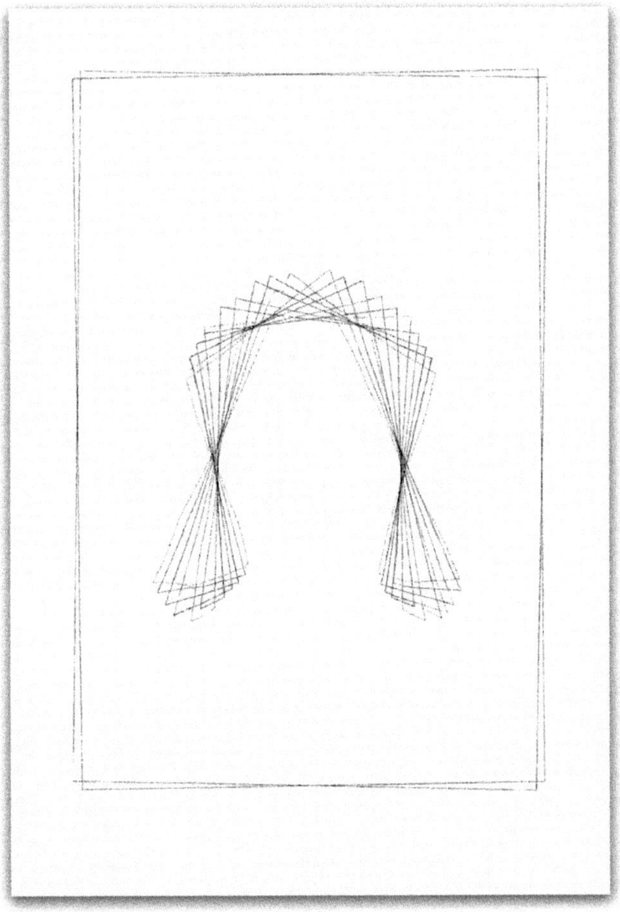

*Threats arrive through voices and screens.*
*They do not belong to my immediate life.*
*Still, the body responds.*

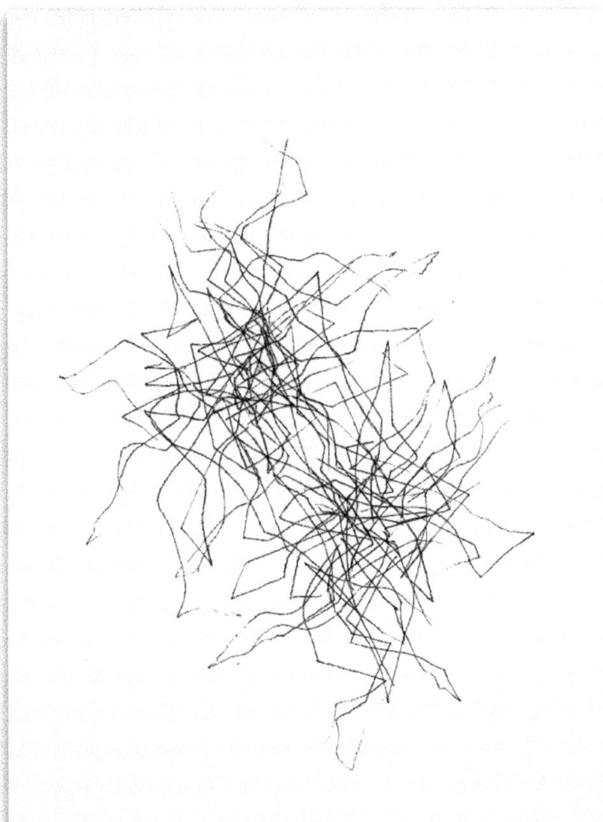

*I learn to hide whole feelings.*
*Something uneasy remains.*
*It has no name.*

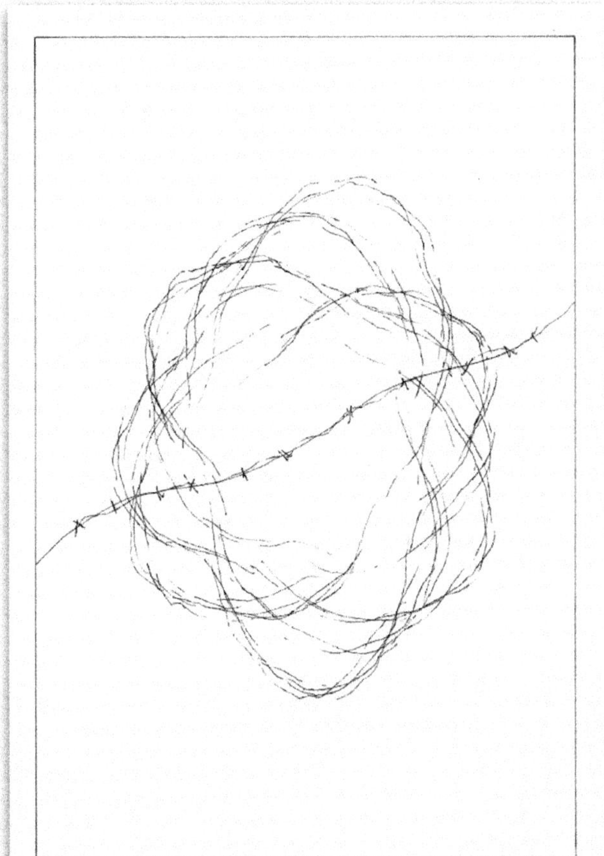

*The unease looks for an enemy.*
*It moves outward.*
*The source stays unfound.*

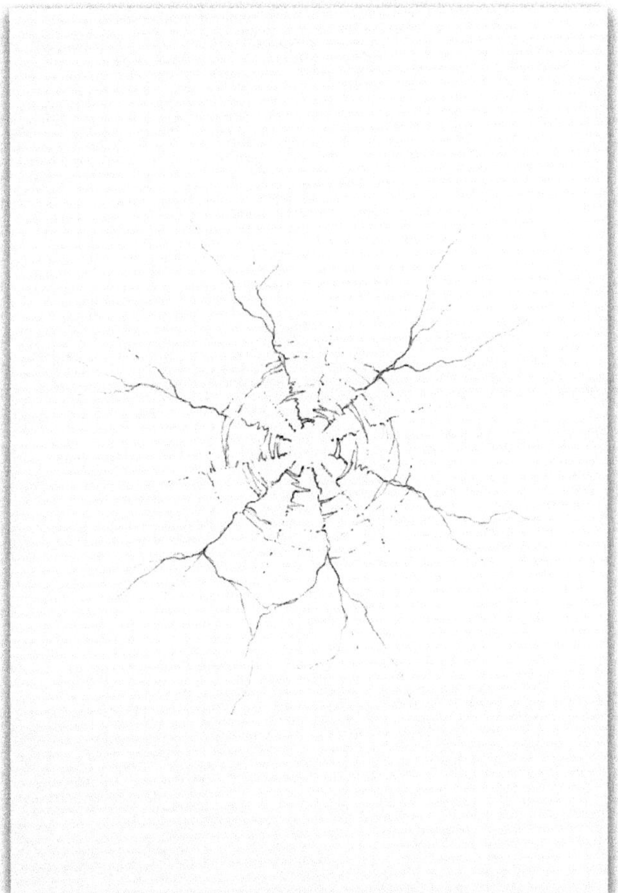

*Raised around anger, the world feels unsafe.*
*The body learns first.*
*Understanding comes later.*

*Low worth twists into comparison and proving.*
*I watch it move through rooms and systems.*
*The pattern repeats without pause.*

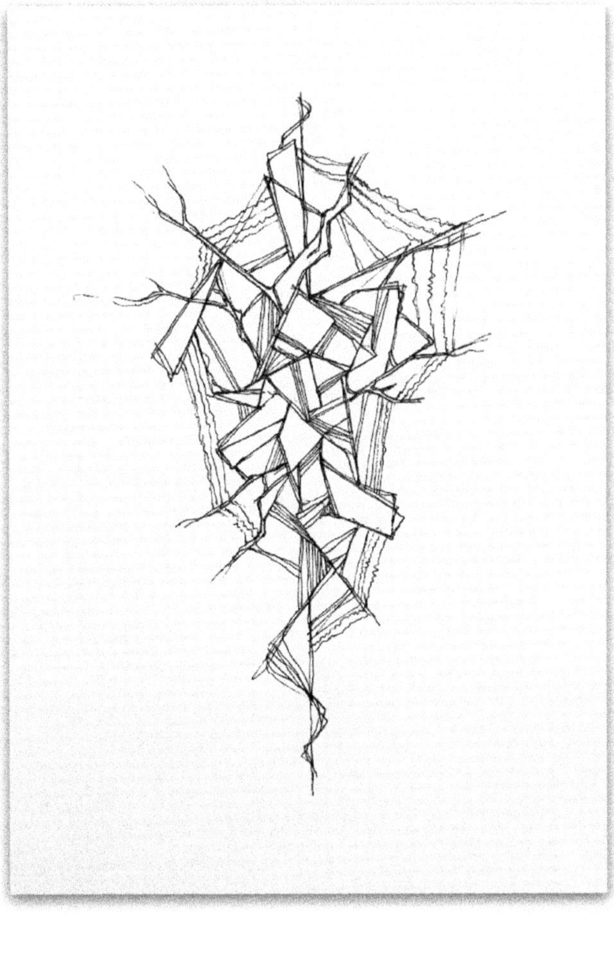

*The danger feels vast and distant.*
*It does not belong to me alone.*
*Still, I carry its weight.*

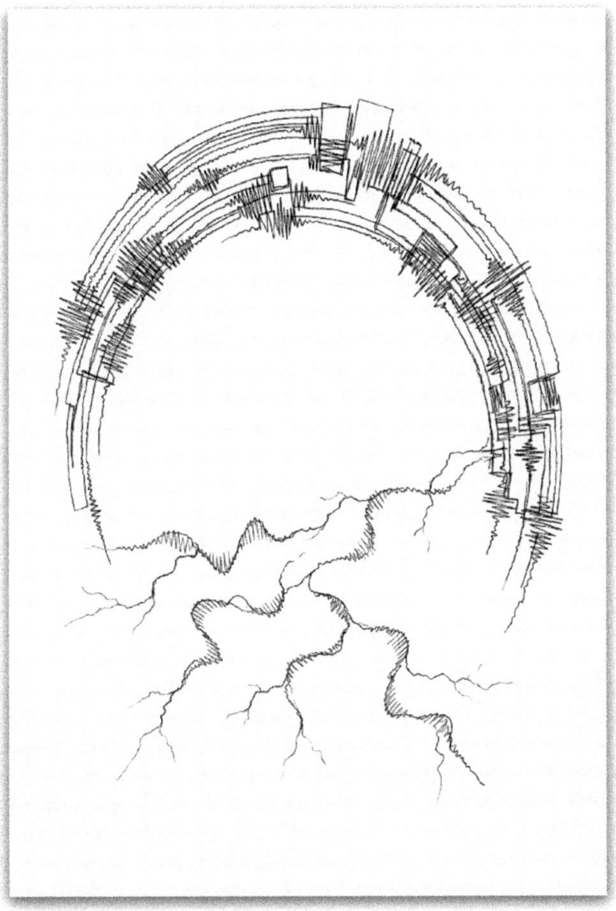

*The reaction begins before awareness.*

*The body moves.*

*The explanation follows later.*

*I go back to the distant inner room.*

*I remain outside it.*

*Distance holds.*

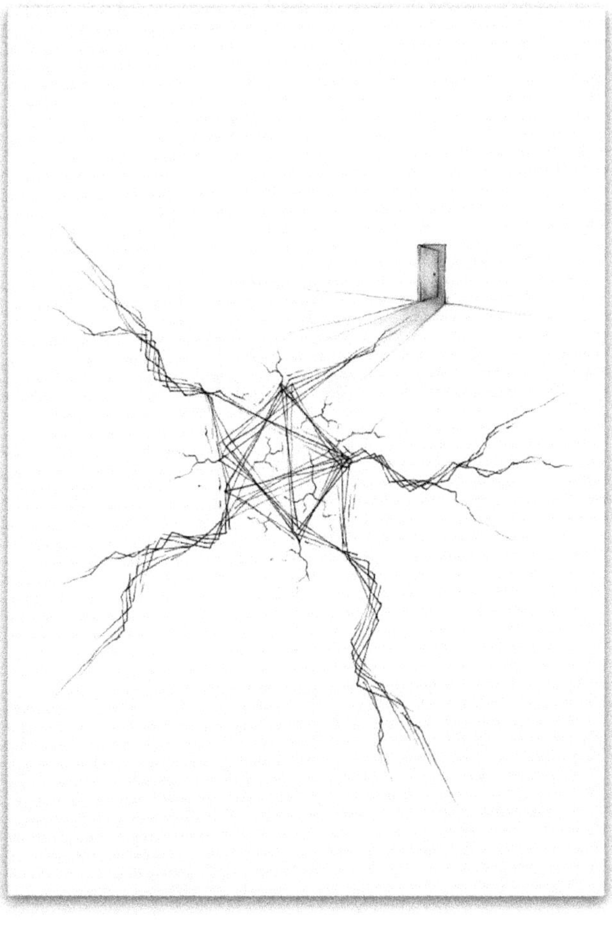

*I hold the memory like an object.*
*It takes on a colour.*
*No explanation arrives.*

*I send it away.*
*Attention turns elsewhere.*
*What happens next is unseen.*

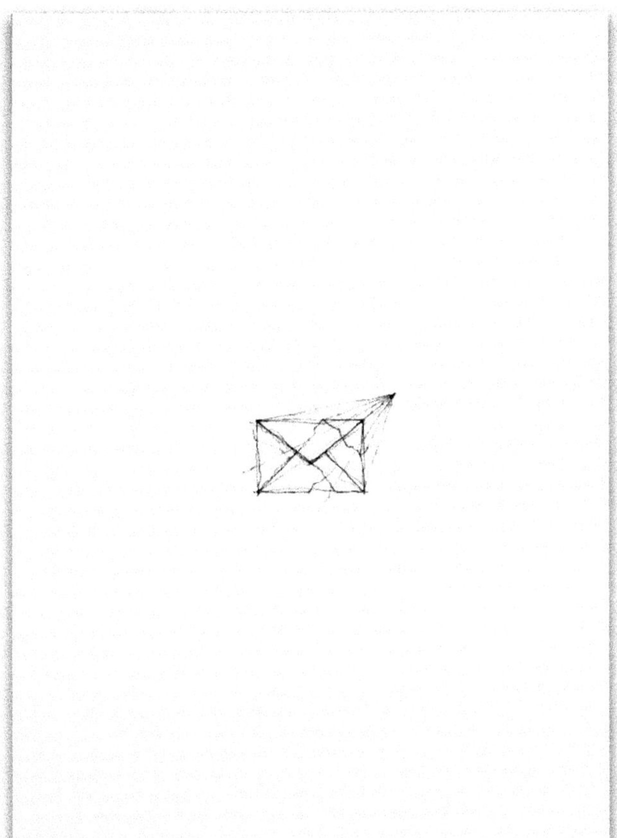

*When it returns, it may be altered or the same.*
*Sometimes it only repeats.*
*I notice what I notice.*

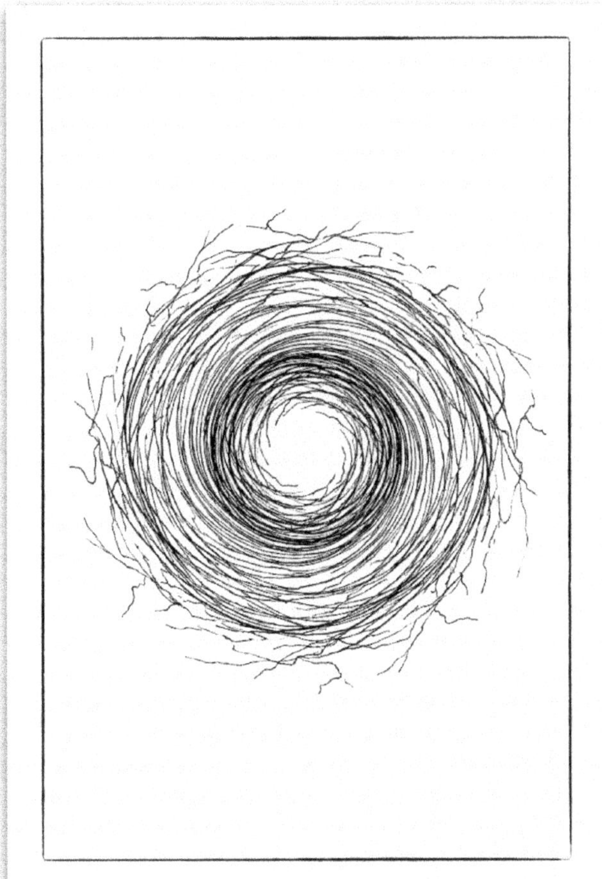

# Chapter 3

*The world is complex enough that threat becomes background noise.*
*I notice how easily "normal" includes tension.*
*The ceiling feels low, even when nothing is happening.*

*There was a time when faith in myself acted like shelter.*
*Then something in me learned too much, too quickly.*
*A door inside me closed without sound.*

*I feel my attention turning away from what disturbs me.*
*The turning-away happens almost by itself.*

*Something obvious becomes unseen.*

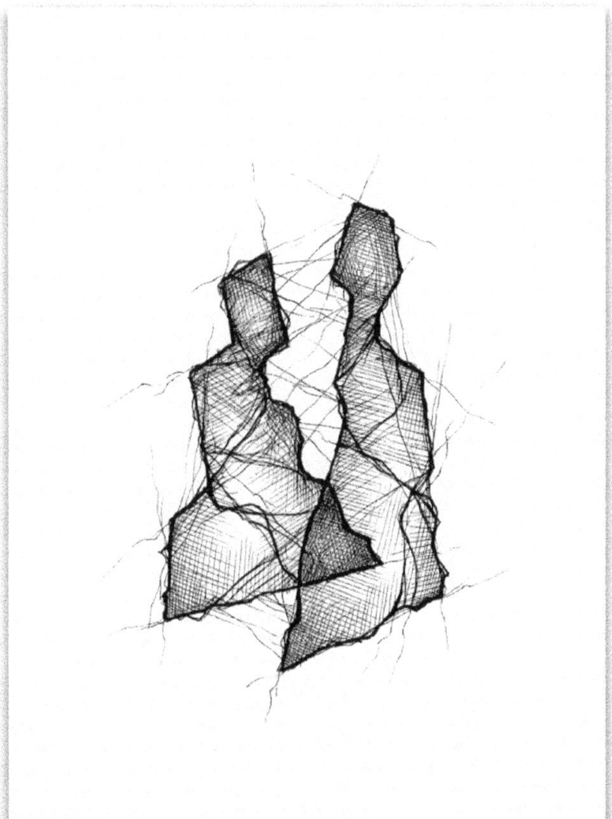

*Thoughts continue.*
*Feeling disconnects.*

*I am present, and not present, at once.*

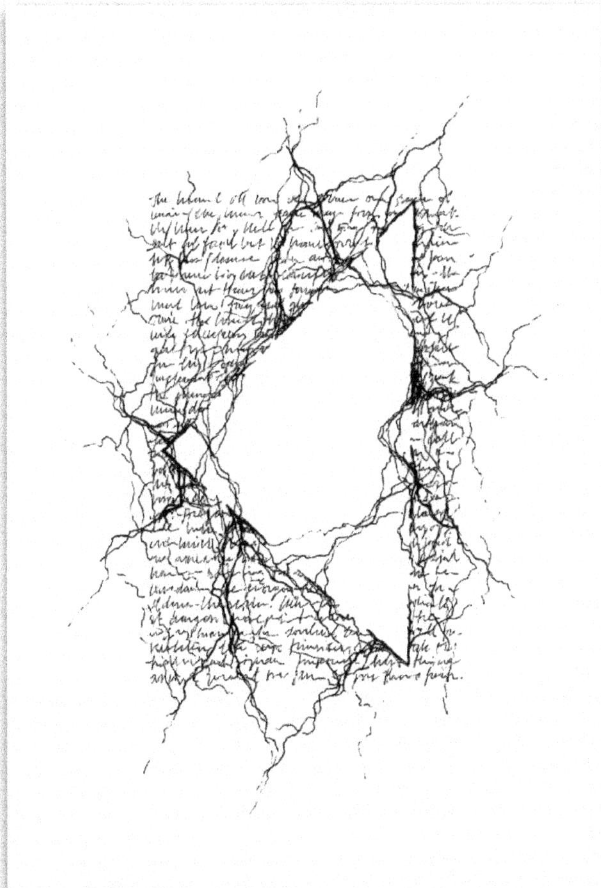

*Fear rises without an object.*
*Then I fear the fear itself.*
*The loop tightens quietly.*

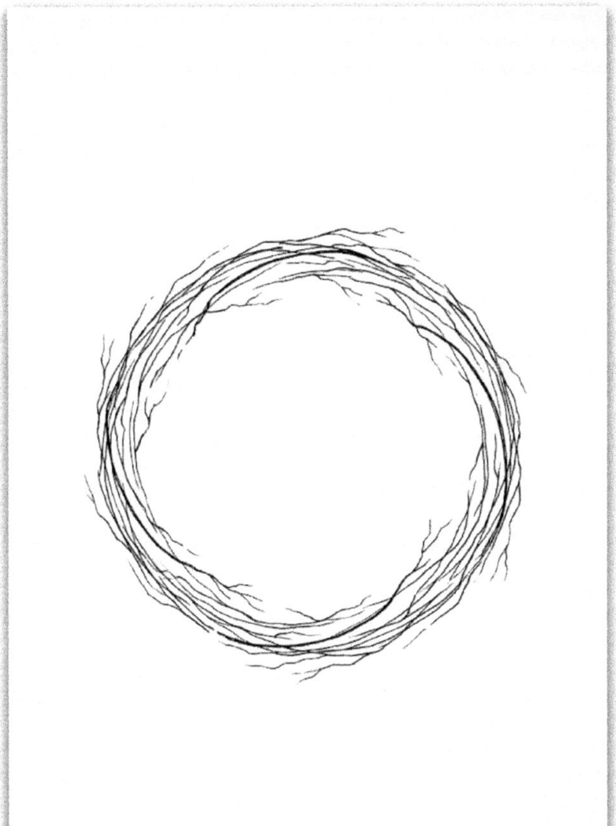

*My life contracts as if the outside has become too much.*
*Distance forms between me and ordinary places.*
*I watch the world from farther back.*

*Tension spills into the body.*
*Aches, fatigue, shifts I cannot map.*
*The body becomes another source of alarm.*

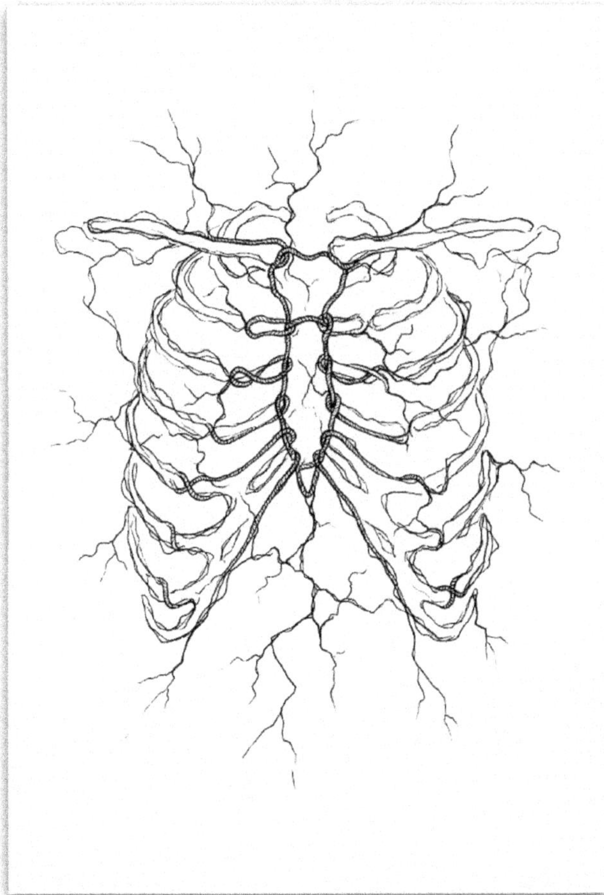

*When what I feel can't be easily explained, I sense judgement in the room.*
*The air hardens.*
*I become smaller inside it.*

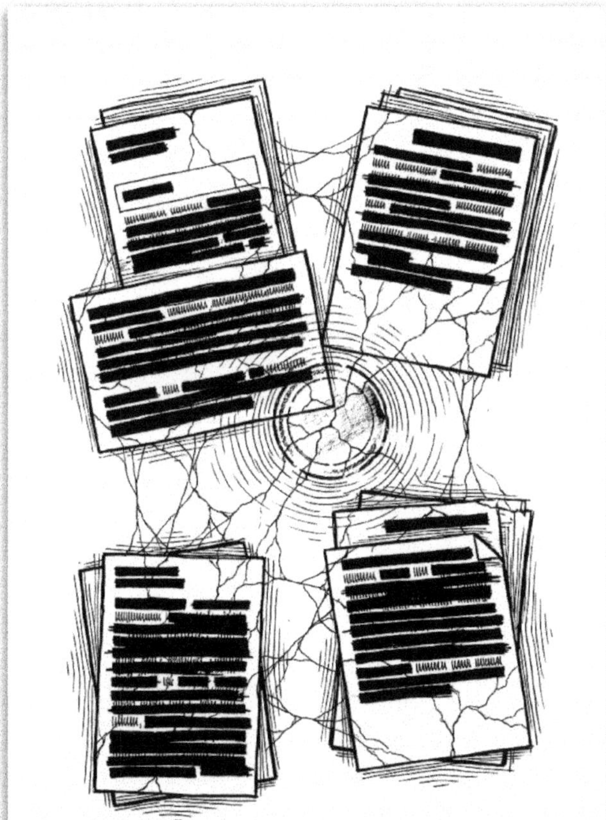

*I return to the idea of processing without being present.*

*Distance becomes the safety.*

*The room stays untouched.*

*I locate my past as a direction in space.*
*It stretches away like a path.*
*I can feel its distance without entering it.*

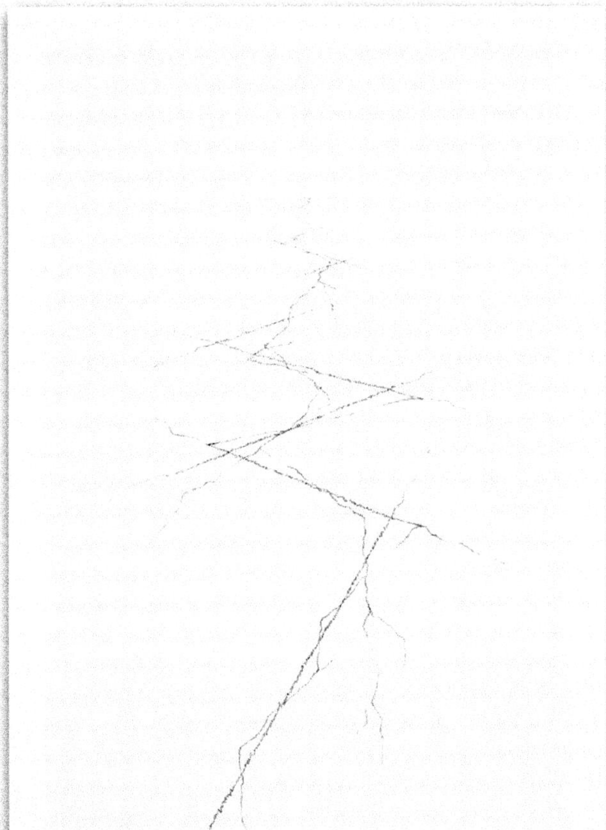

*The past appears as sealed cases.*
*Some feel familiar; some are blank.*
*Certain clusters call louder than others.*

*I move steadily, collecting without opening.*
*The motion is simple.*
*The contents stay unseen.*

*I arrive at a beginning so early it feels like emptiness.*
*I turn and see my whole life laid out as distance.*
*The start is almost blank.*

*On the way back, I notice stray glints left behind.*
*I reach the present again.*
*Changed mainly by quiet absence.*

# Chapter 4

*Something in me stays activated.*
*Even in quiet moments, the body doesn't fully settle.*
*After the impact, the tremor continues.*

*The unexpected presence of another person hits like danger.*
*The body reacts before meaning arrives.*
*I register it as closeness, not as a thought.*

*Social threat lands like a physical sting.*
*A look can feel like a verdict.*
*A small exile, without movement.*

*Safety begins to feel conditional.*
*I measure myself against rules that keep shifting.*
*The scale never rests.*

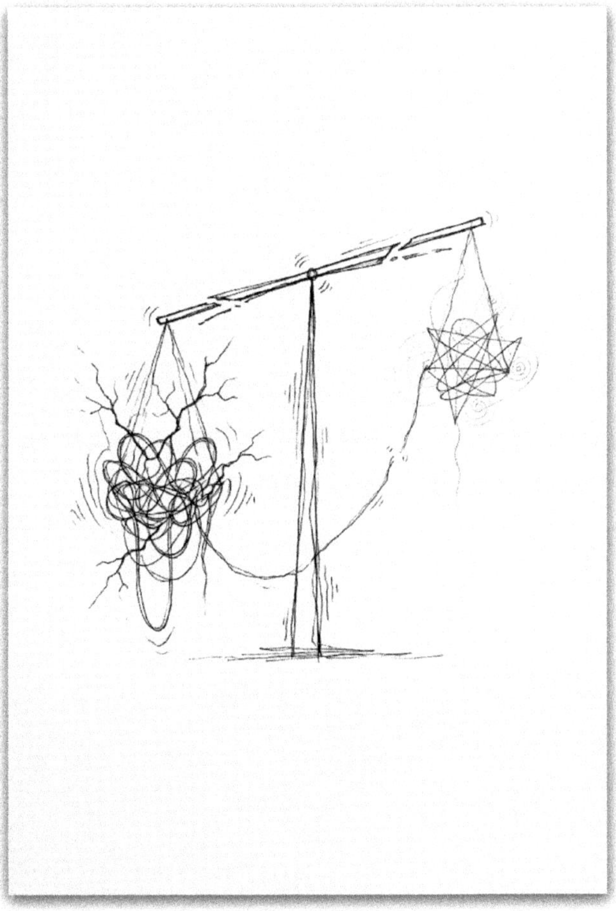

*I remember arranging and repeating.*
*Small orders that made the world feel manageable.*
*The relief was real, even if brief.*

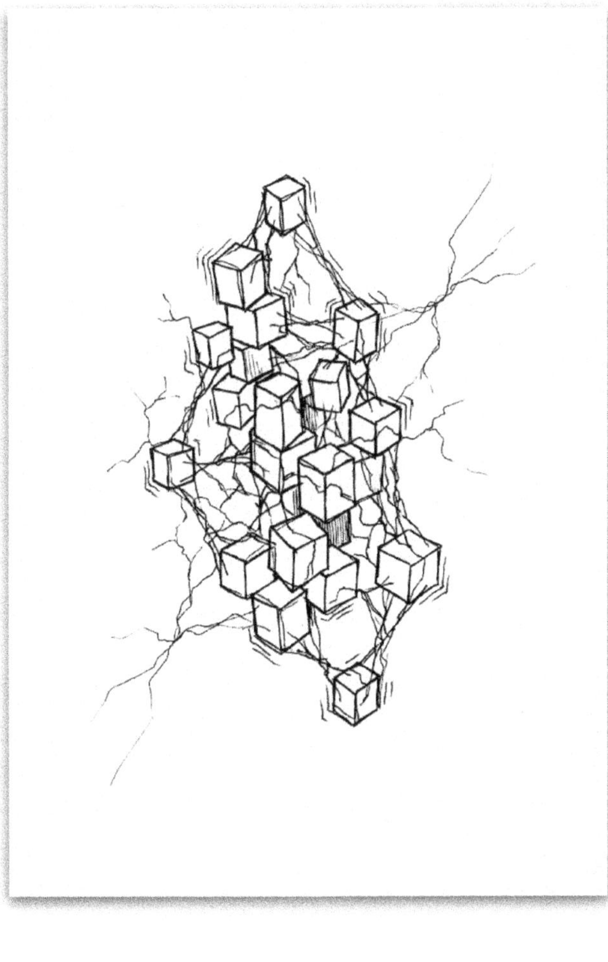

*The same tension can branch in different ways.*
*Numbness. Agitation. Meticulous control.*
*Three doors from one corridor.*

*Sometimes force looks like strength and gets rewarded.*
*Under it, something trembles.*
*The surface holds; the seam shows.*

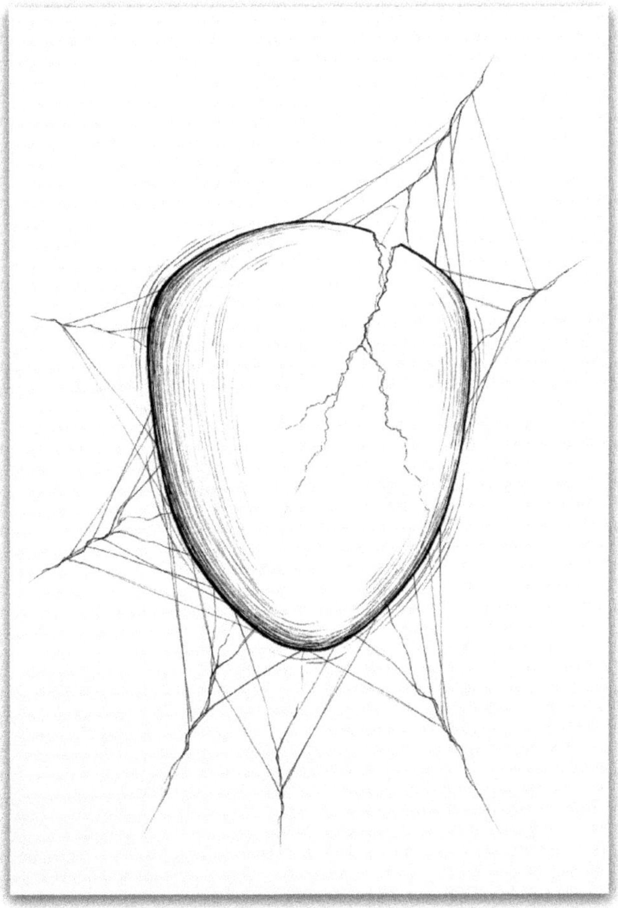

*Images and messages make me feel smaller than I was a moment ago.*
*The pressure is ambient, not chosen.*
*It arrives as atmosphere.*

*Instead of fleeing the surge, I notice it.*
*A thin thread of curiosity stays present.*
*The movement continues, and I remain near it.*

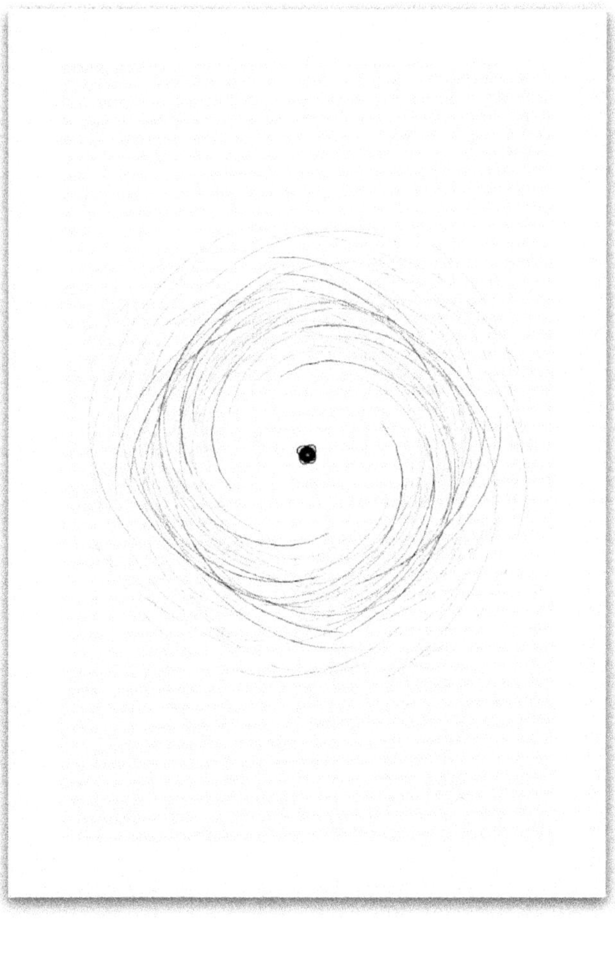

*I sense the approach before it arrives.*
*The question comes first.*
*Then the body answers.*

*I face the future as a simple road.*
*It stretches out, quiet, slightly descending.*
*Nothing happens yet.*

*Something begins to form ahead.*
*Bright, sealed, not yet understood.*
*I meet it as an object, not a story.*

*At the far end there is emptiness and distance.*
*I look back and see my life as one long line.*
*The shape is simple from here.*

*From distance, judgement loosens.*
*Something like warmth falls without selecting.*
*The return is quieter than the leaving.*

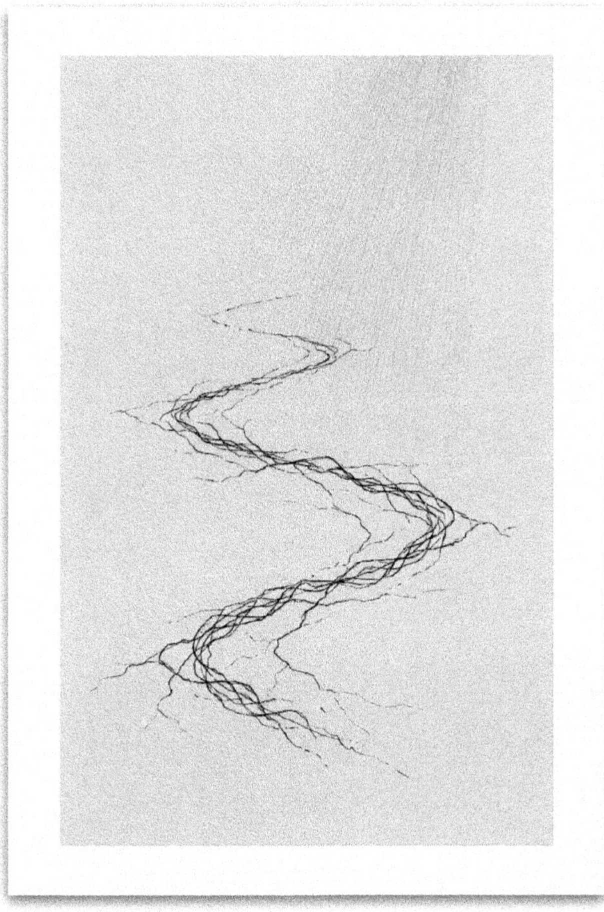

# Chapter 5

*I hold the word nemesis and feel it like a bell in the chest.*
*Not a rival.*
*Something woven into me.*

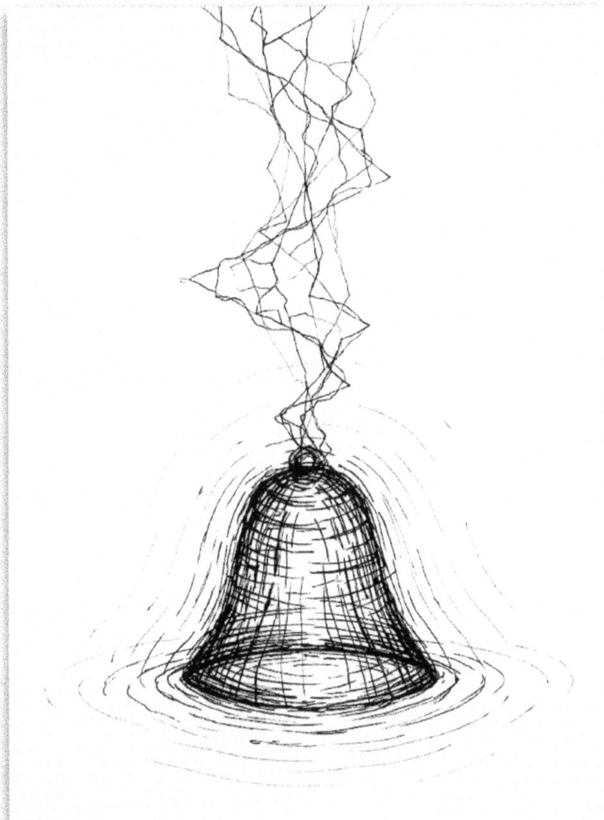

*The reaction happens first.*
*I arrive after it, trying to catch up.*
*The story comes late.*

*The sense of one self isn't as solid as it feels.*
*Different voices carry different memories.*
*I notice the overlap.*

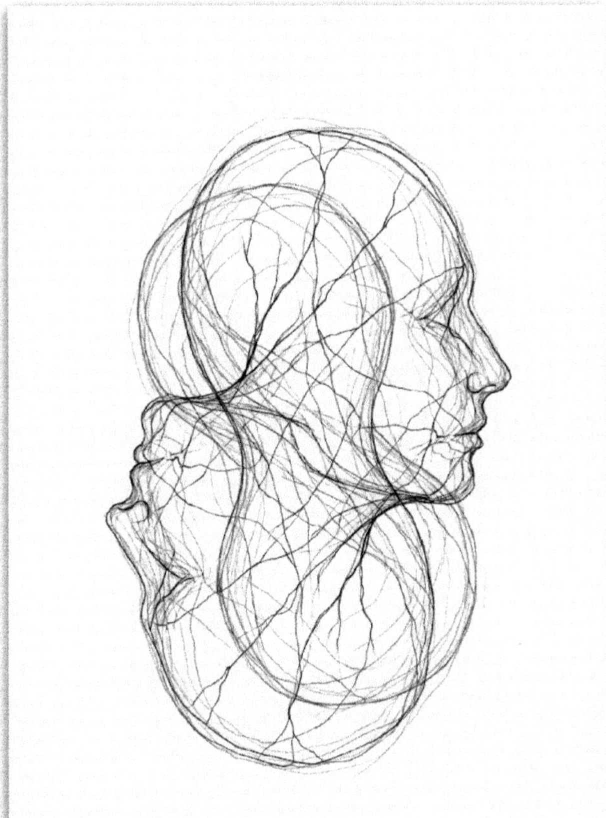

*A name gathers stories around it.*
*The stories start to feel like a fixed person.*
*The label holds.*

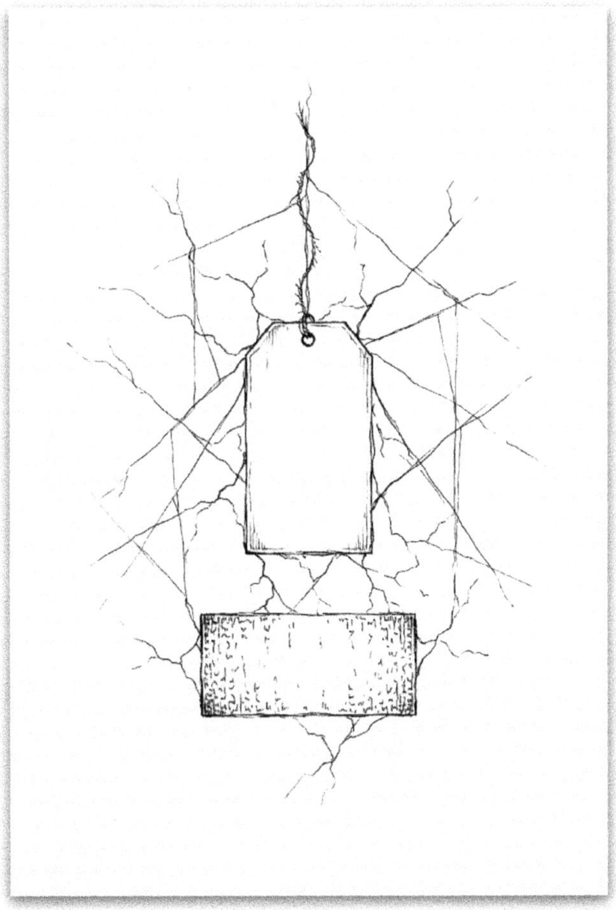

*I can be certain I lack confidence.*
*The contradiction sits quietly.*
*Unquestioned.*

*To keep one story about myself, I exile what doesn't fit.*
*Certain moments are hidden away.*
*The drawer stays shut.*

*I sense a companion made of what I refused to be.*
*It waits in the margins.*
*Not speaking.*

*The mind divides: good/bad, us/them, right/wrong.*
*The edges feel clean.*
*Until they don't.*

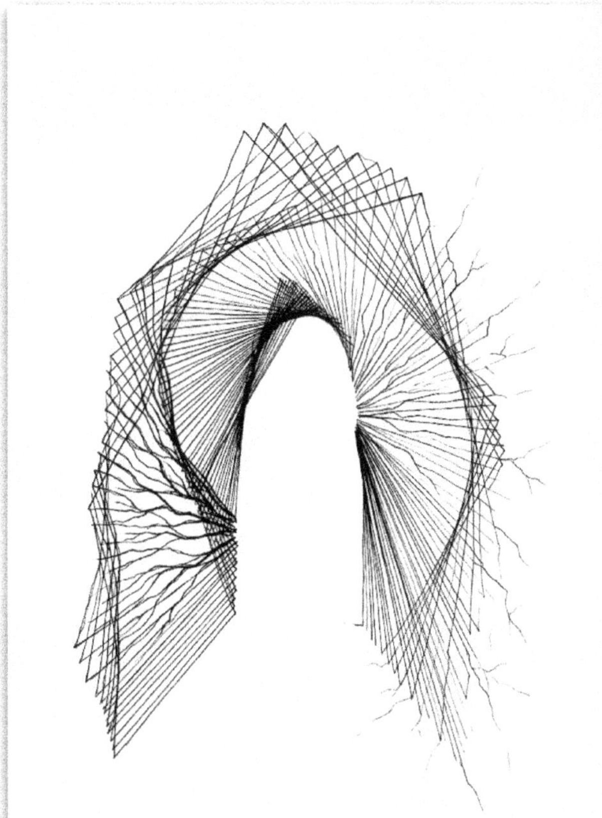

*Old judgements remain attached to memories.*
*The label outlives the moment it named.*
*I feel the mismatch.*

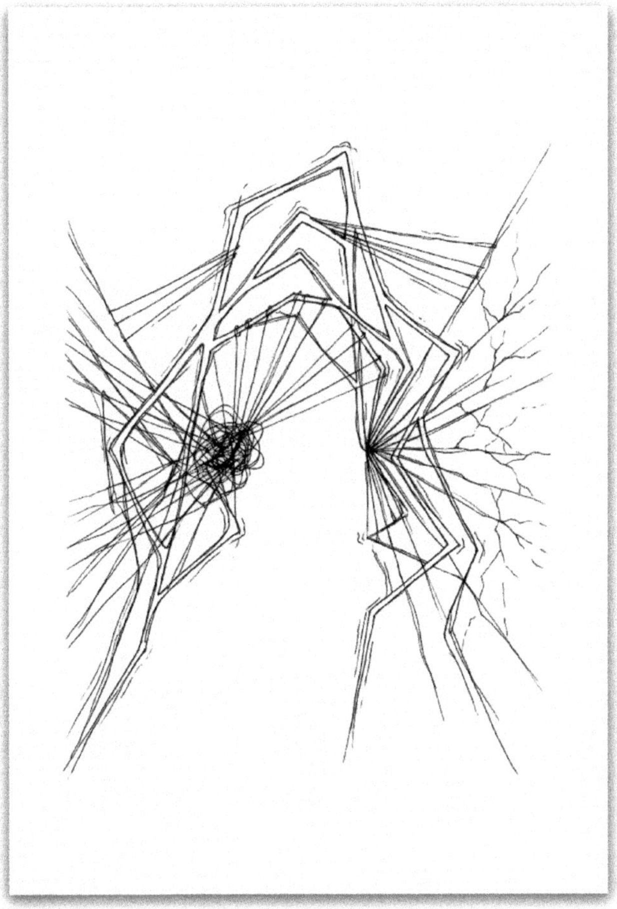

*Behind the dread is an ending I can't negotiate with.*
*A horizon that doesn't move.*
*No drama—just distance.*

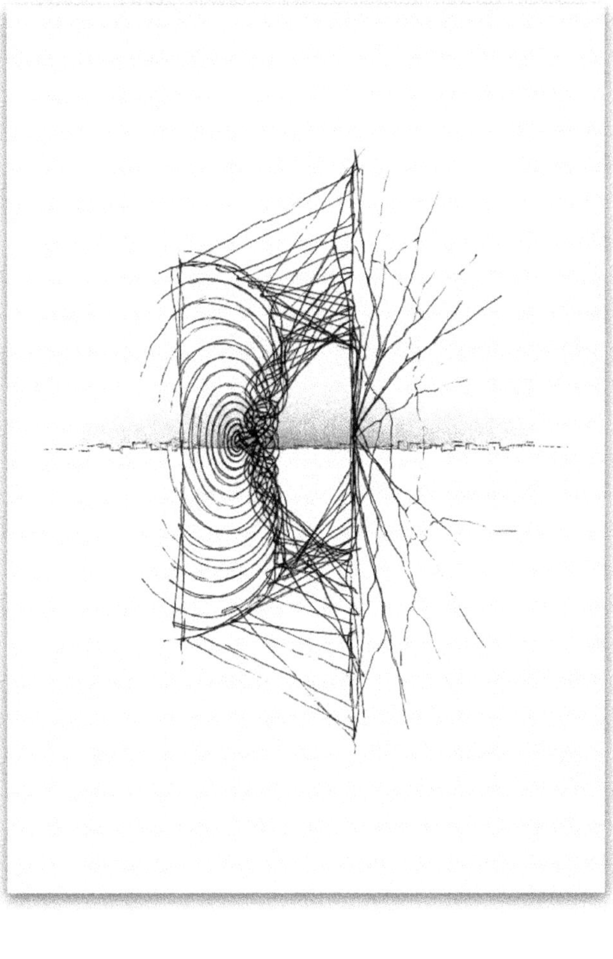

*I imagine the final exhale.*
*And the stillness after.*
*The urgency loosens.*

*From that far place, my life becomes a single line.*
*The harsh verdicts don't follow me here.*
*Only the shape remains.*

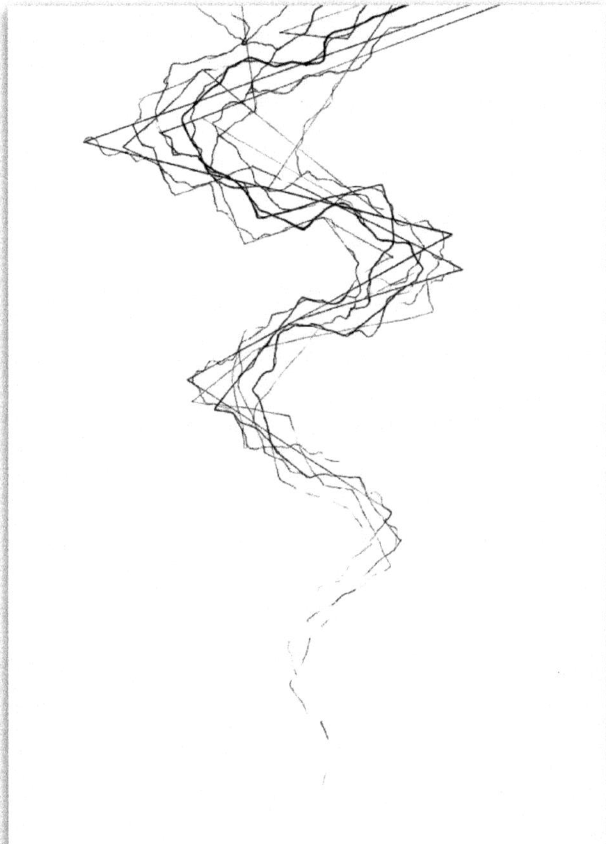

*I include the companion-self I hid from.*
*Like recognising a face I've avoided.*
*No ceremony—just contact.*

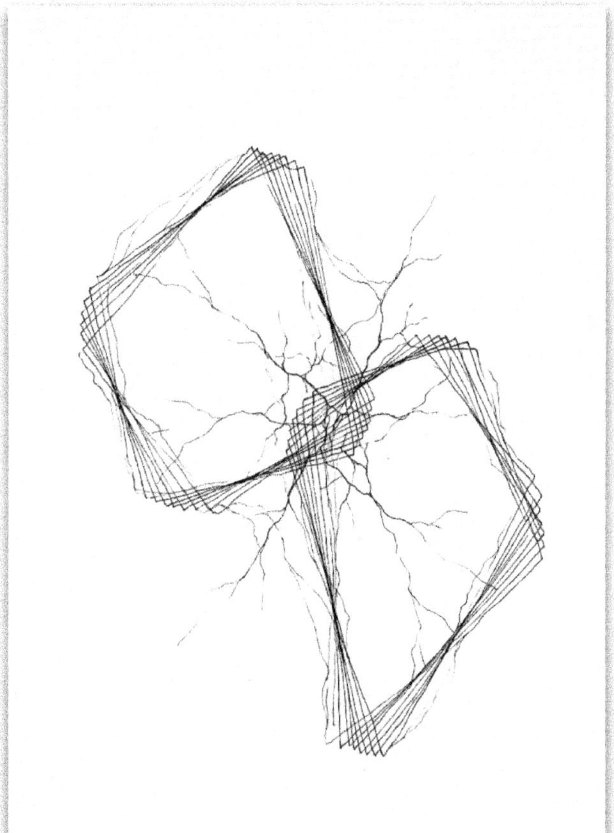

*A warm centre in the chest comes back with me.*
*Not triumph.*
*Just a steadier heat.*

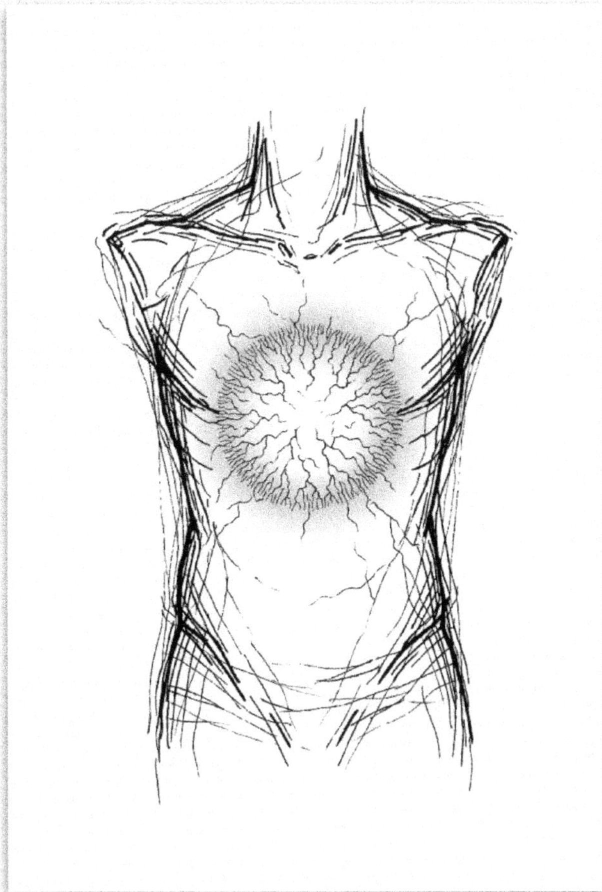

# Chapter 6

*My attention latches onto sensations that don't need to be foreground.*
*The noticing itself becomes loud.*
*Even quiet becomes busy.*

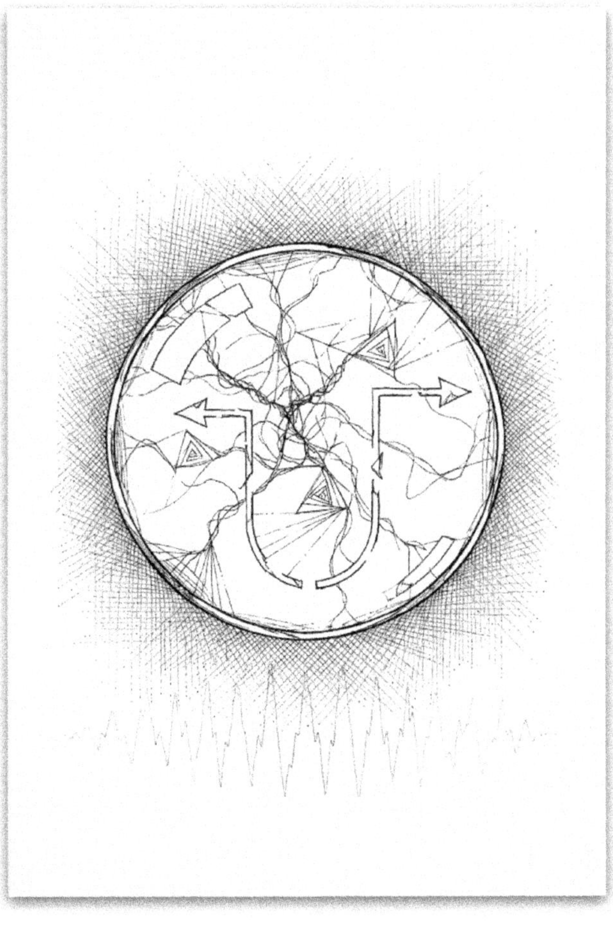

*I sense different layers moving at once.*

*Raw perception, thinking-feeling, and the story of "me."*

*They don't always agree.*

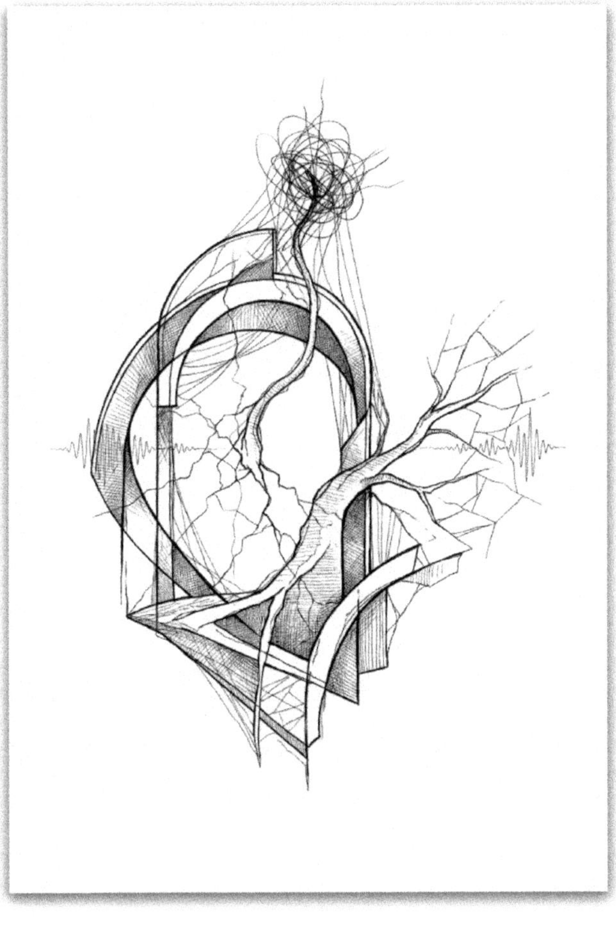

*Everything gets split into opposites.*
*I feel the slice: up/down, good/bad, me/not-me.*
*The cut happens quickly.*

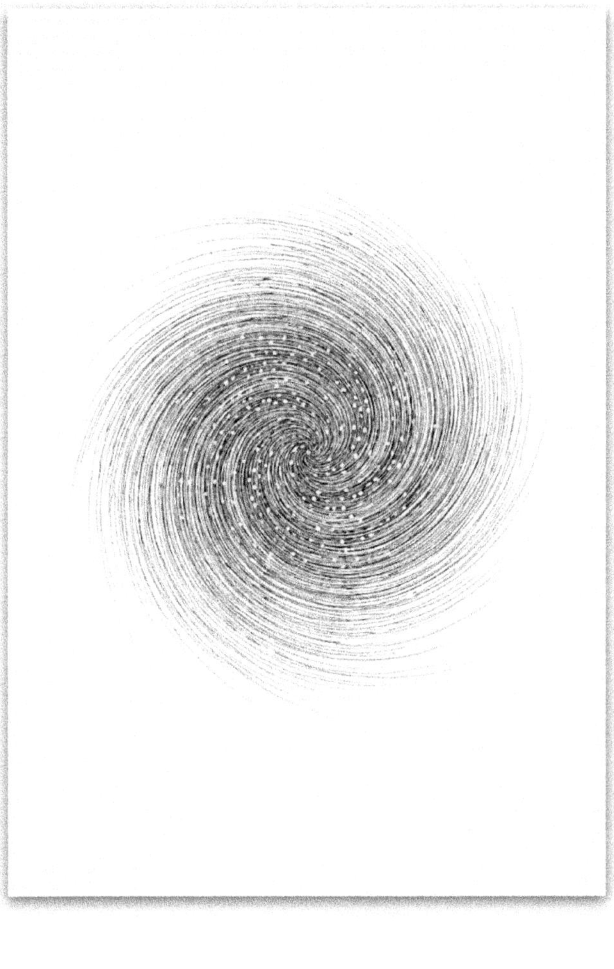

*I move through life as if it's ordinary.*
*A brief shock of wonder appears.*
*Then it fades again.*

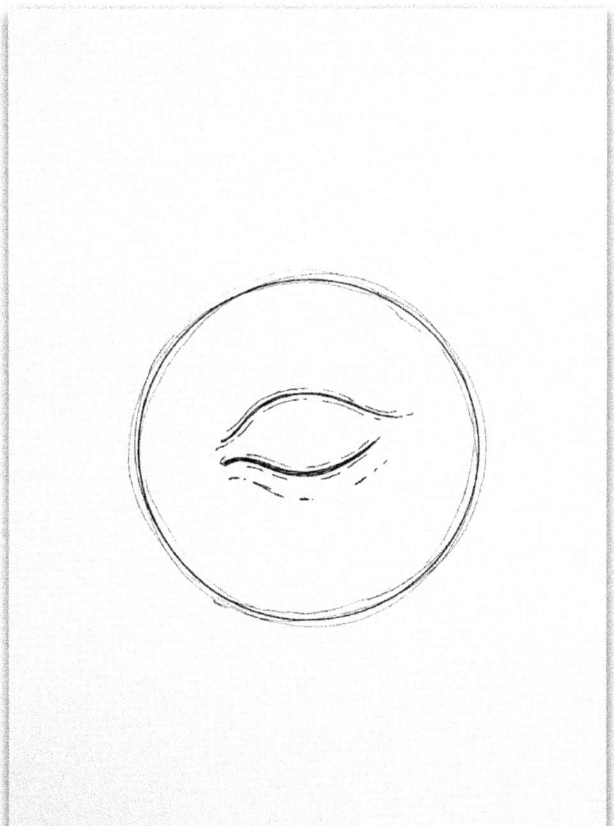

*In dreams I shift places without question.*
*The "I" becomes thin.*
*Time bends easily.*

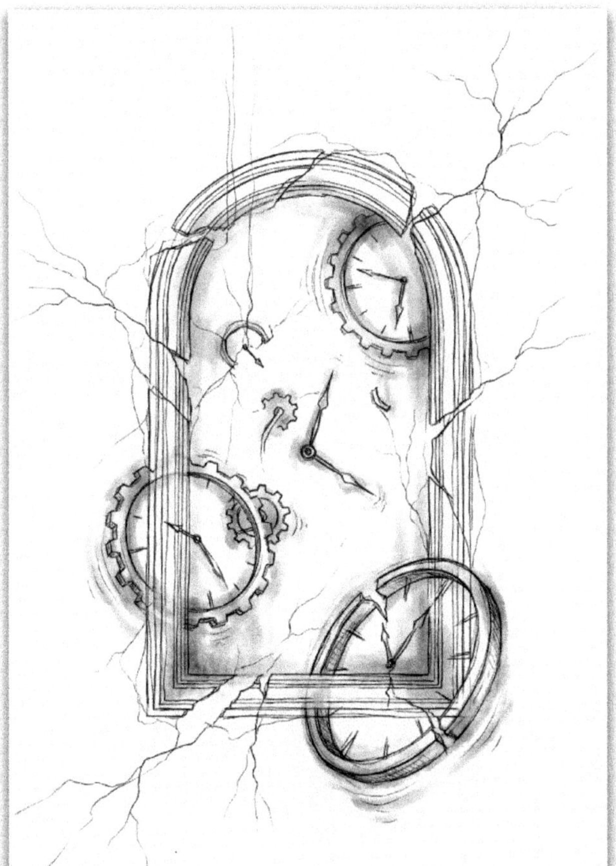

*There is a blank depth I barely recall.*
*It feels like being without story.*
*Nothing to explain.*

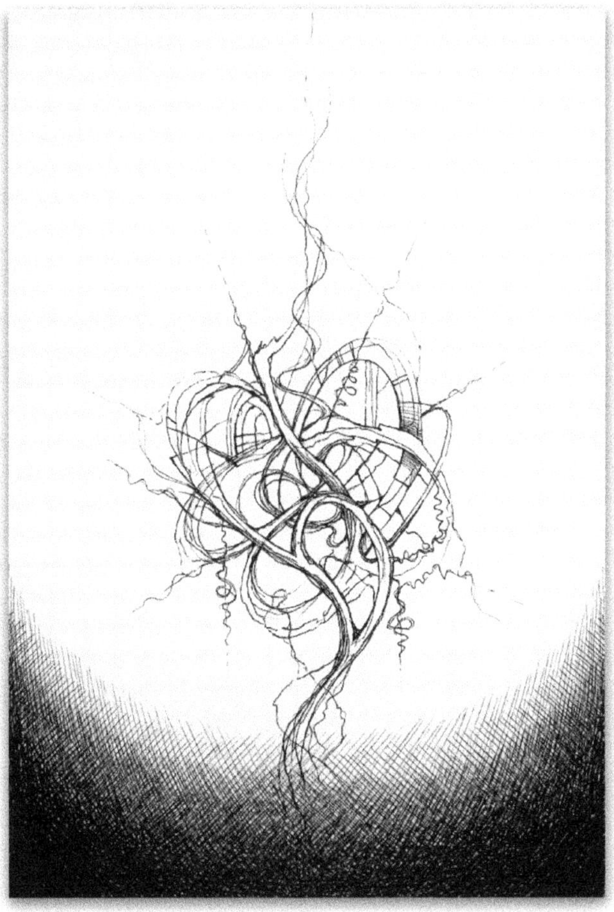

*I imagine a depth beyond the shoreline mind.*
*Out there, separateness doesn't hold in the same way.*
*The image arrives, then withdraws.*

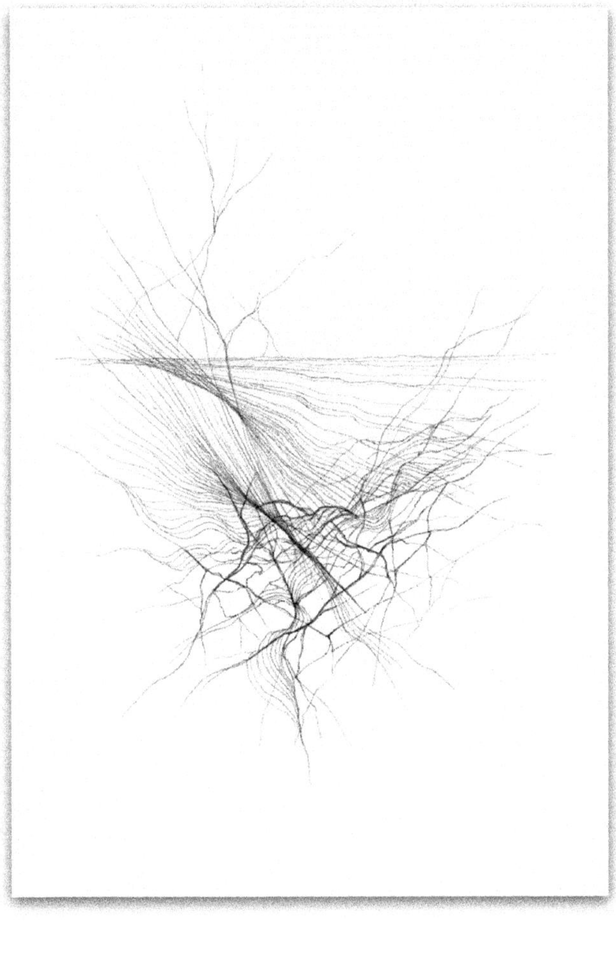

*When I can't properly switch off, I wake un-restored.*
*It's as if the night never fully happened.*
*The day begins already used up.*

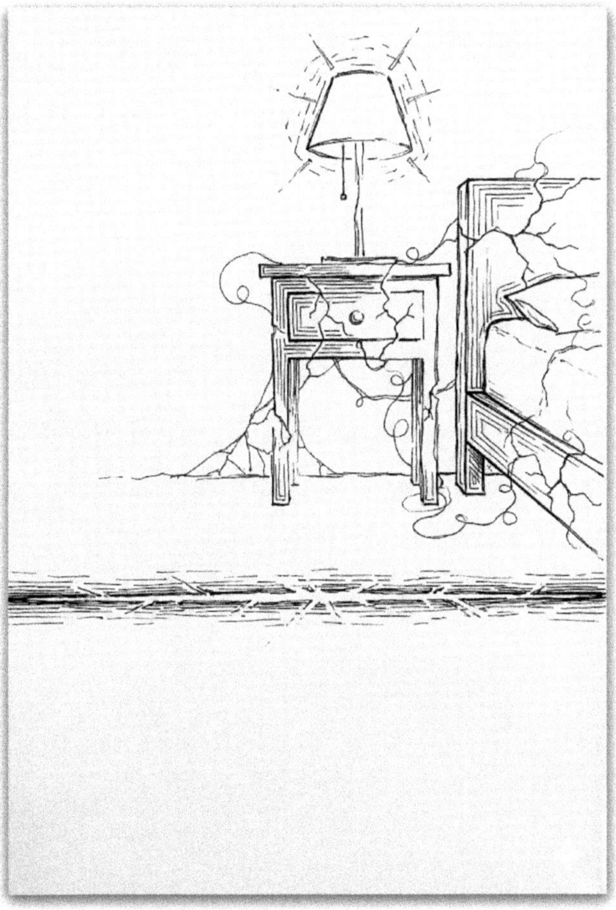

*Sometimes I forget who I am for a moment.*
*Movement, rhythm, task—nothing else.*
*The relief is wordless.*

*When I try to inspect myself with the mind, it multiplies.*
*I get caught in reflections of reflections.*
*The centre keeps shifting.*

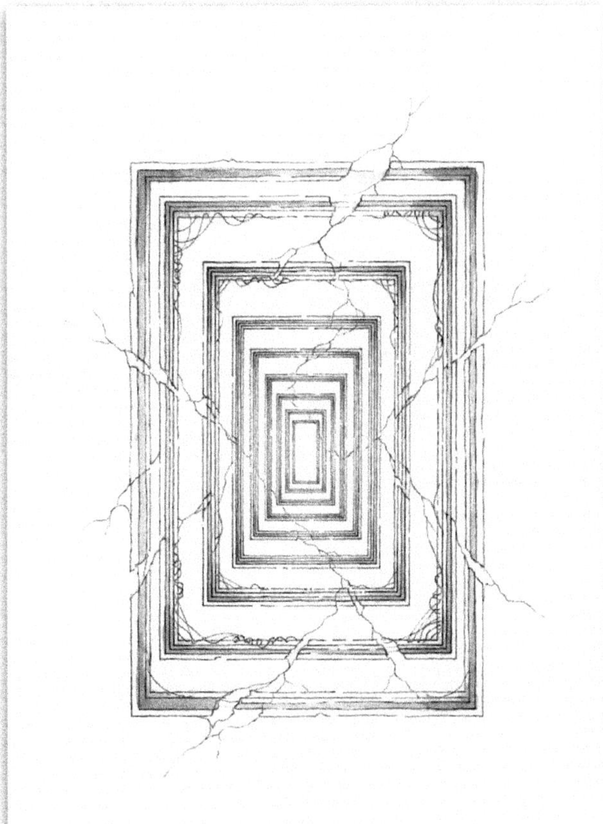

*I look for something and miss what's in front of me.*
*The search brightens and narrows the scene.*
*The obvious stays unregistered.*

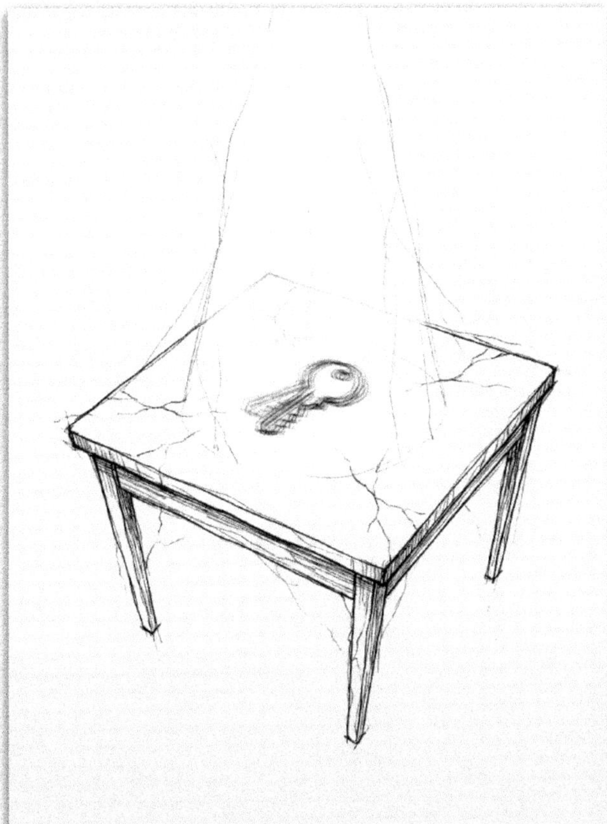

*What I refuse in myself feels like it moves outside me.*
*The world becomes charged with that refusal.*
*I notice the charge without naming it.*

*To say I don't want something, I still picture it.*
*The thought arrives wearing a minus sign.*
*The image remains visible.*

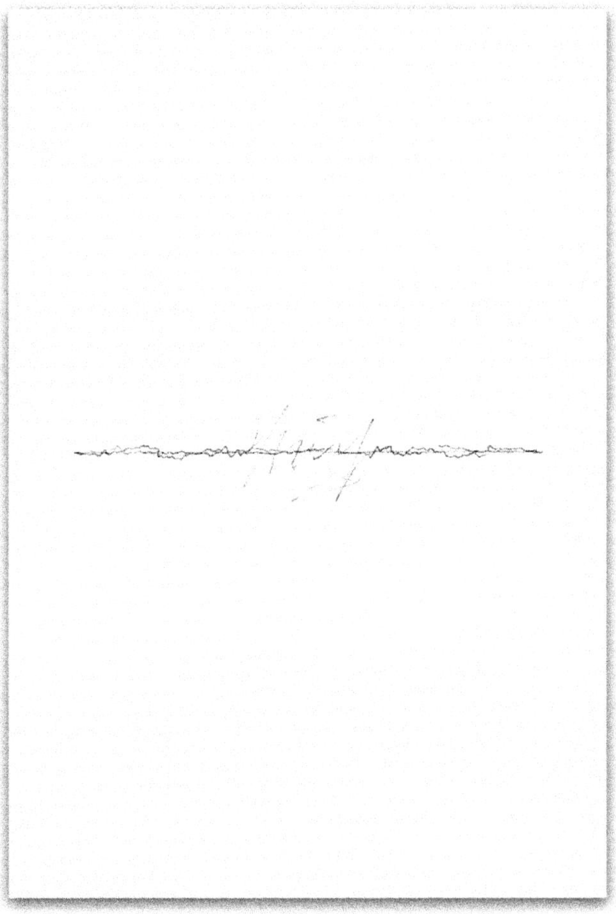

*I ask the question and watch answers fall away—*
*name, role, story.*
*The words loosen.*
*What remains is quiet and unclaimed.*

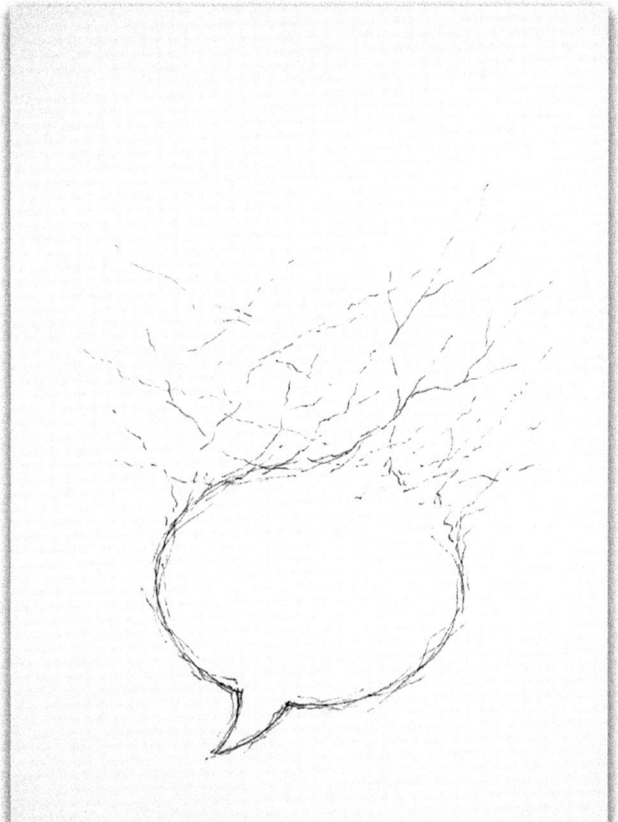

# Chapter 7

*I picture a code born from violence, and the quiet tenderness that sometimes follows it. The image arrives without instruction. Something in me leans toward it, not for strength, but for order after fear.*

*Fear feels like heat. Not metaphorical, but bodily—pressure and narrowing. Whatever passes through it is changed, marked by the temperature it endured.*

*The word lands awkwardly. Not triumph. More like a description of cost. Something worn daily, unseen, under ordinary clothes.*

*There is a giddy edge where fear and power mix. It can look like confidence. From the inside it feels unstable, as if one movement too far would scatter it.*

*I notice how often I rehearse the ending. Over time it loses drama and becomes familiar, almost ordinary—another object in the room.*

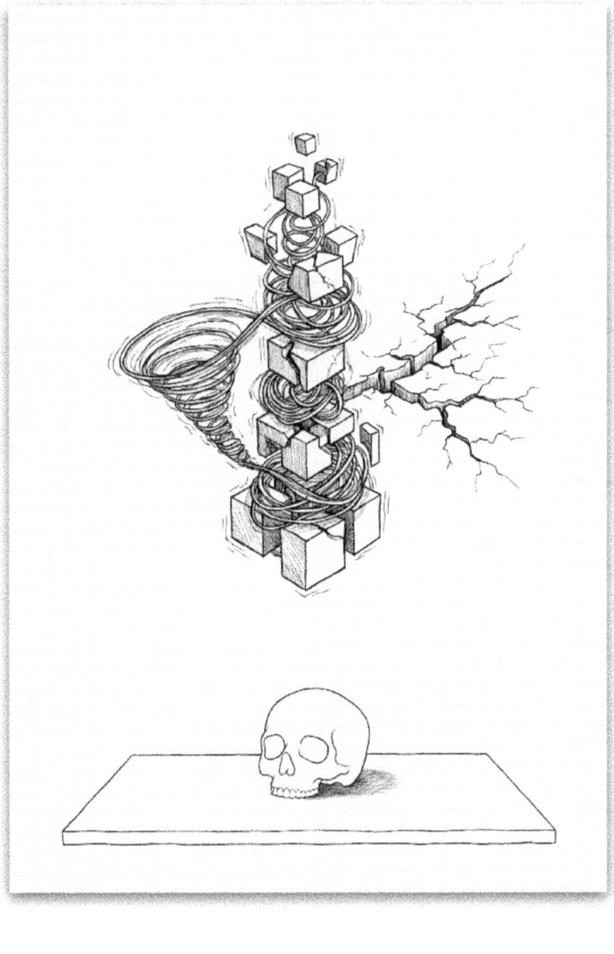

*Behind the noise, something quieter is already there. It does not argue. It arrives before sentences form.*

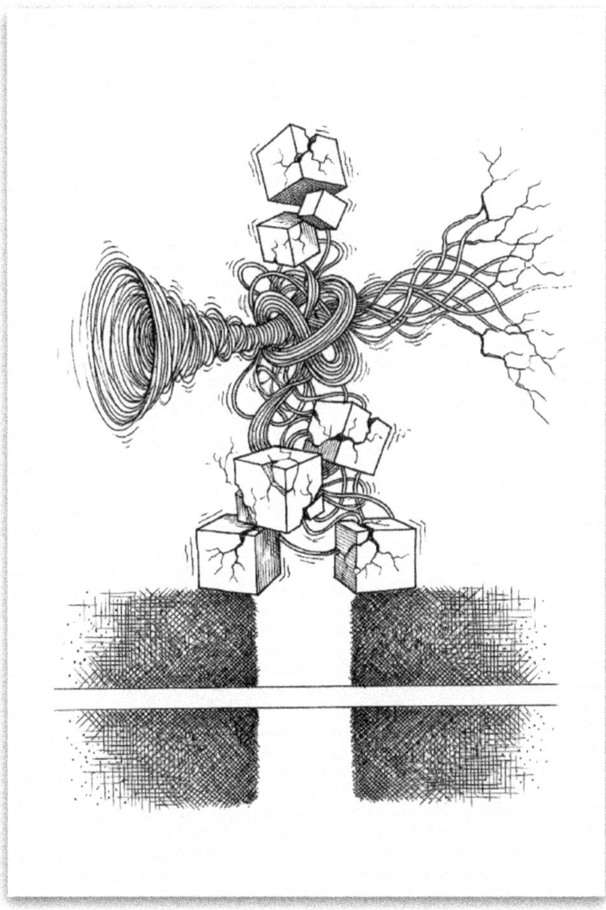

*I sense that nothing is lost. Even what I call forgotten waits intact. A small cue can open the whole room again.*

*When a thought appears, a watcher seems to appear with it. I cannot tell which comes first. They rise together, inseparable.*

*For a brief moment, things unfold without commentary. No manager arrives. Movement happens, then rests.*

*Some thoughts speak as if they are not mine. The tone is familiar, sharp, intimate. I listen without answering.*

*When I do not feed the thought, it changes. It does not vanish. It loosens.*

*I face a blank wall. My eyes move inward, awkwardly. Balance has to be learned, not forced.*

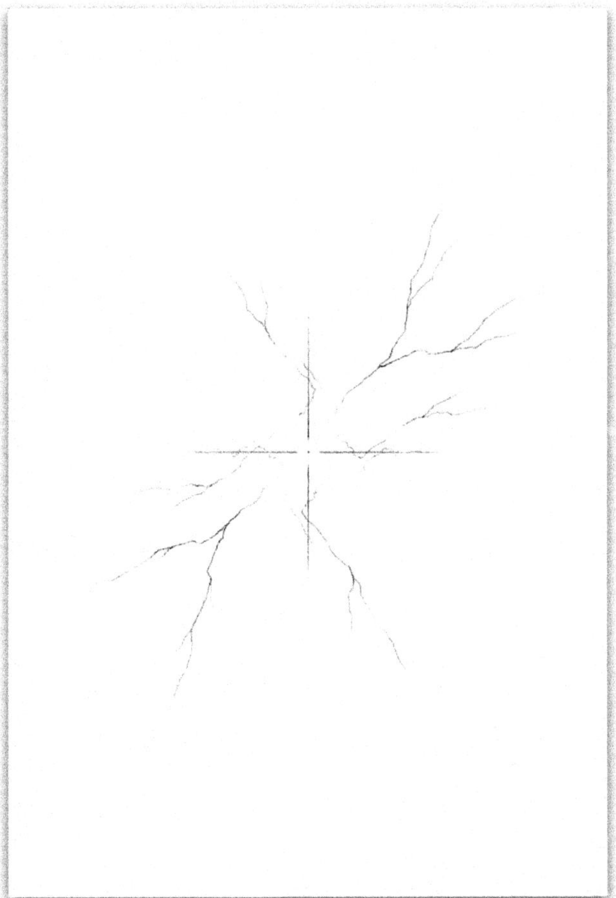

*Two halves meet. A small pyramid appears, an X at its tip. Symmetry settles the field.*

*Something like an eye surfaces on the blankness. It startles, then becomes just another appearance.*

# Chapter 8

*I look back and realise I've been carrying this longer than I admit. There's a quiet fatigue in it. There's also a quiet pride—not triumph, just the fact of endurance.*

*Something rises in me fast—heat, tightening, a quick inward flinch. I watch it arrive without needing to name it, as if it is simply weather moving through the room.*

*I stay with the sensation instead of stepping away from it. It feels less like bravery and more like holding position—still, attentive, without a story about winning.*

*It isn't one breakthrough. It's the same small return, again, in ordinary moments. The repetition is quiet, almost unimpressive, and that is part of its honesty.*

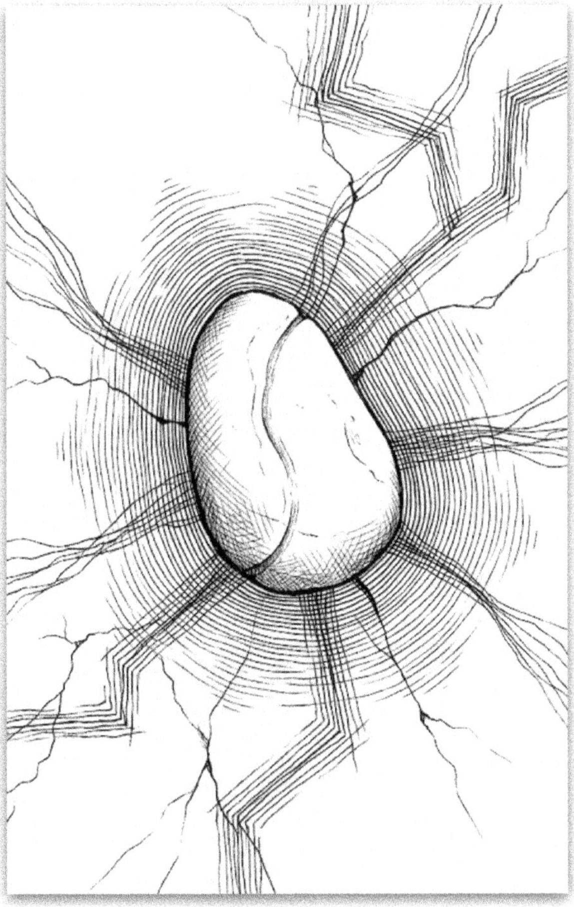

*I feel the heat of being seen. My body tries to fold itself smaller, as if visibility is danger. The urge arrives before any explanation.*

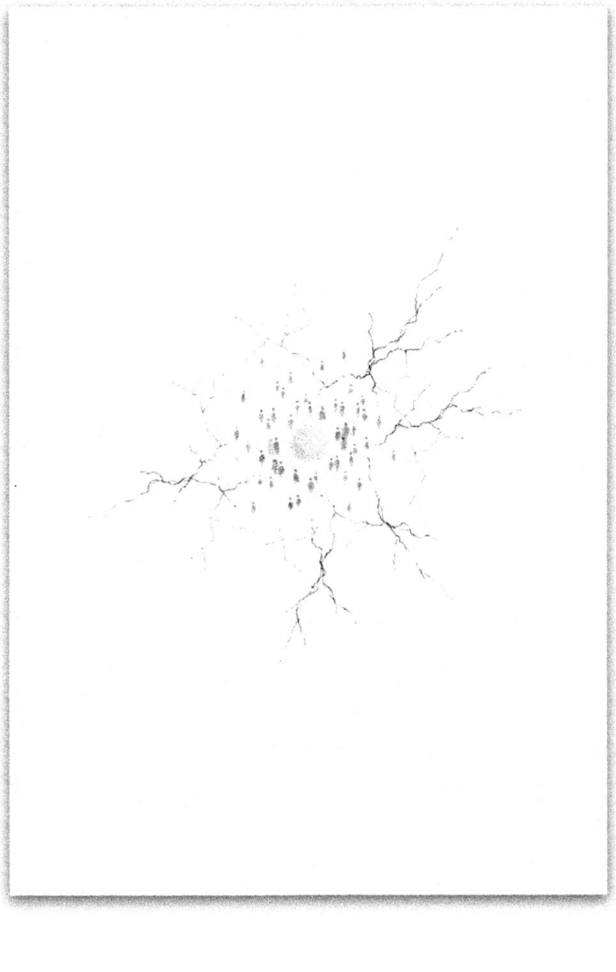

*My mind measures me against others. The measuring makes everything hard. It turns contact into a contest without anyone else agreeing to play.*

*The instinct is to avoid. Under it there is a thin line of willingness—small, not heroic. I notice both at once, and the moment stays unresolved.*

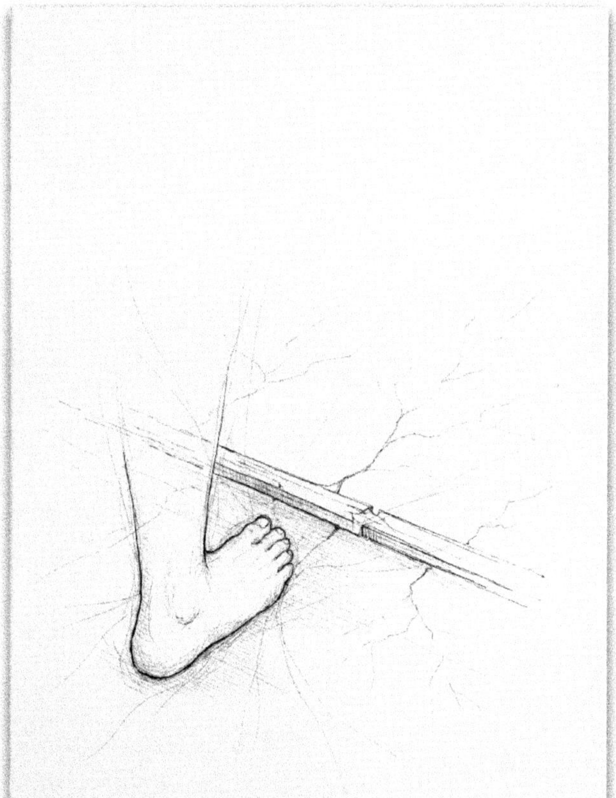

*The same surge can feel like threat, or like brightness. I notice how easily the mind assigns one label and forgets the other.*

*I try on a different name for myself—one that doesn't apologise for how often I've had to meet fear. The name doesn't solve anything. It only holds the shape more gently.*

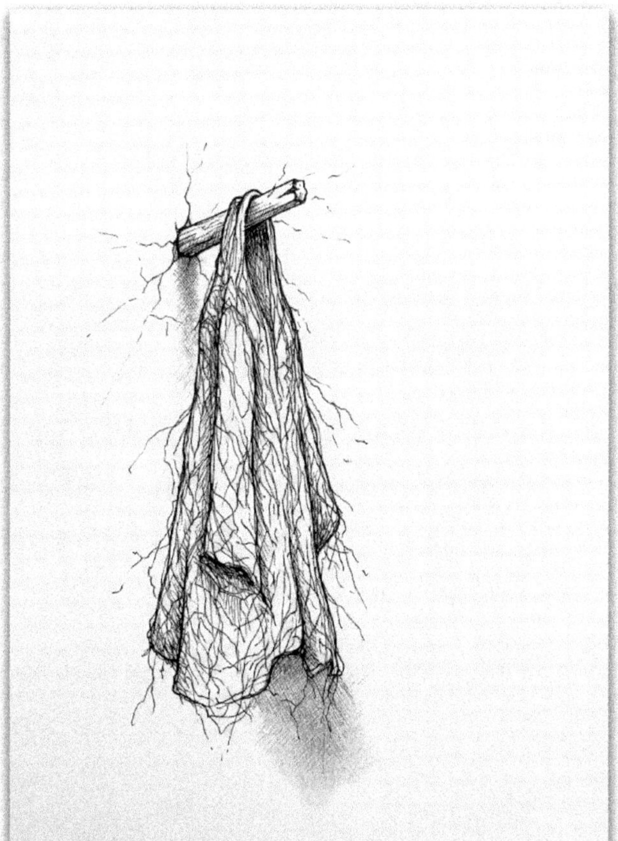

*The thought of the end appears. I don't chase it away, and I don't make it meaningful. It stands there for a moment, like a distant line, then the day continues.*

*I feel how control tightens me—jaw, throat, chest. When the grip loosens, it isn't victory. It's simply a small unclenching, and the room feels wider.*

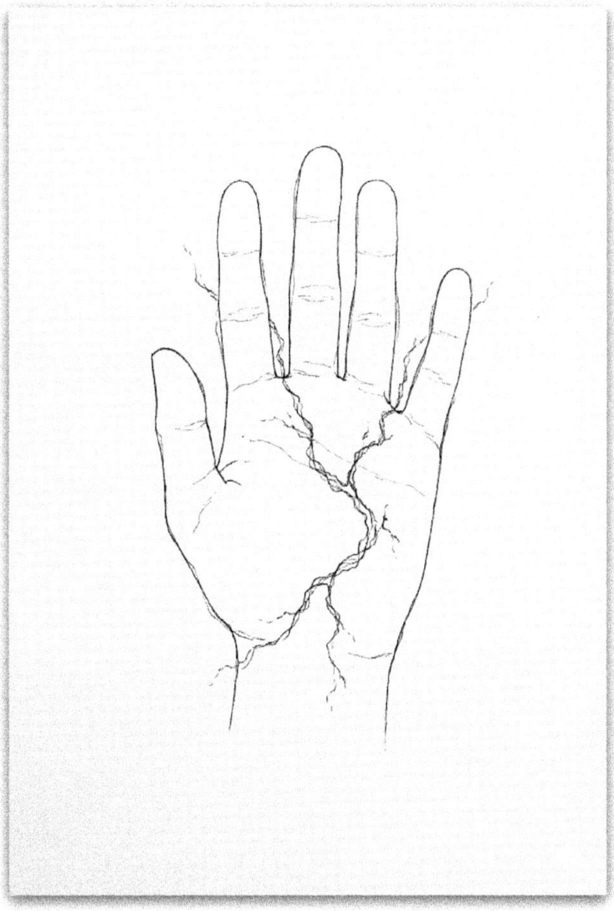

*I sense the weapon I carry and choose not to draw it. The restraint is not moral purity. It's a refusal to turn shame into heat, and heat into harm.*

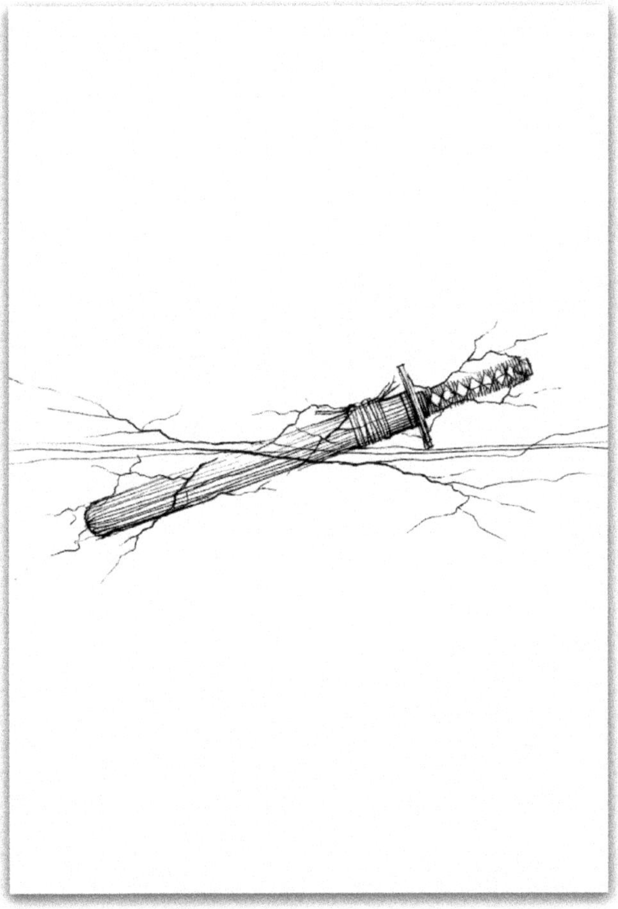

*In the mind's scene I crest a hill and see a figure far below. My pulse lifts. Nothing happens yet. The whole event is the body's quick change in weather.*

*Two vast presences settle at my shoulders—one bright, one dark. They do not speak. The distant threat changes size in my perception until it feels small, almost absurd. Then the road is simply a road again, and I walk on.*

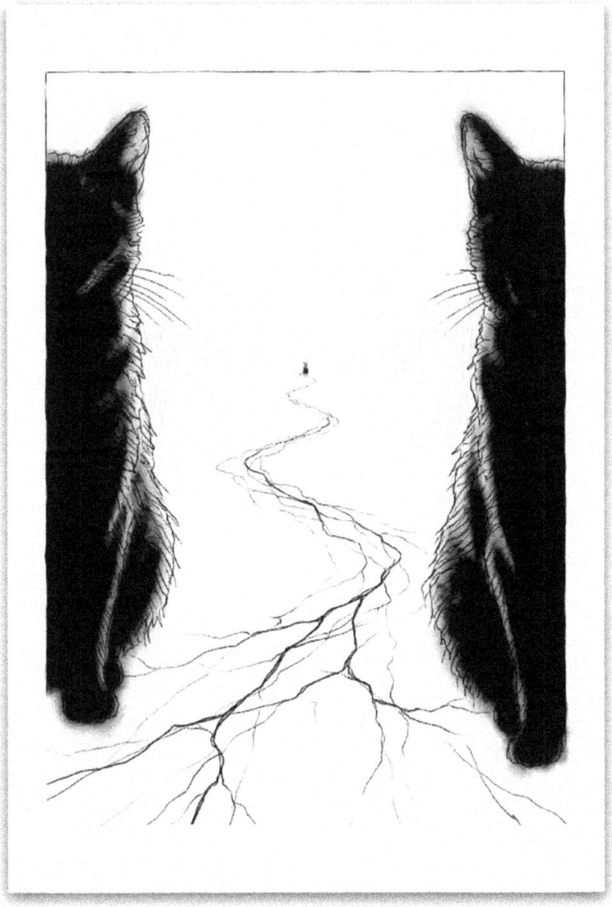

# Chapter 9

*The word lands in me differently than it used to. Less like an ending. More like something opening—quietly, without announcement.*

*I notice the familiar distance: as if I'm behind my eyes, watching the room through a pane. The room is here, and I'm here, but the contact feels filtered.*

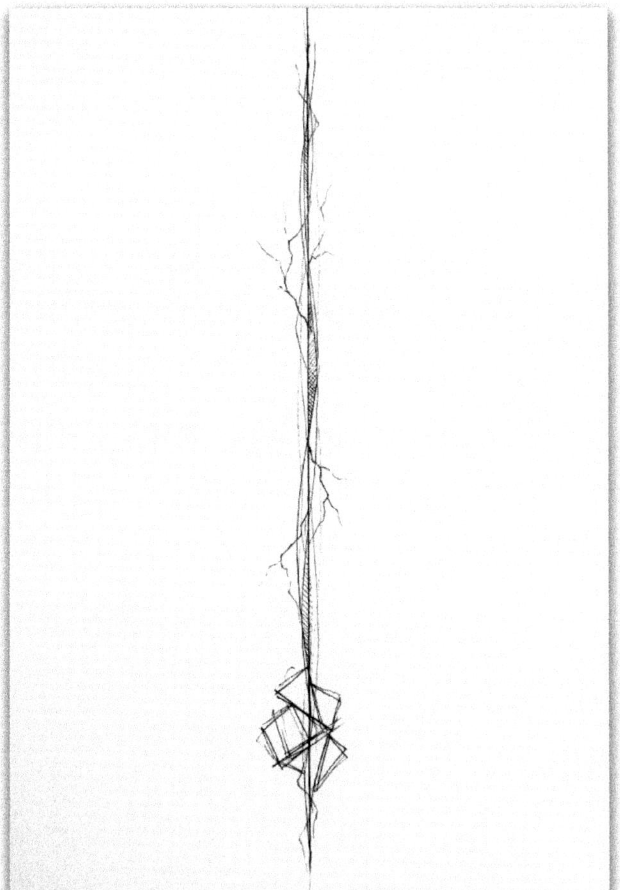

*When I soften, the inner tempo changes. Noise thins—not solved, just less crowded, like a room after people leave.*

*Sometimes the edge of me feels less defined.* Not *ecstasy—just a subtle loosening of separation, as if the body is not as alone as it insists.*

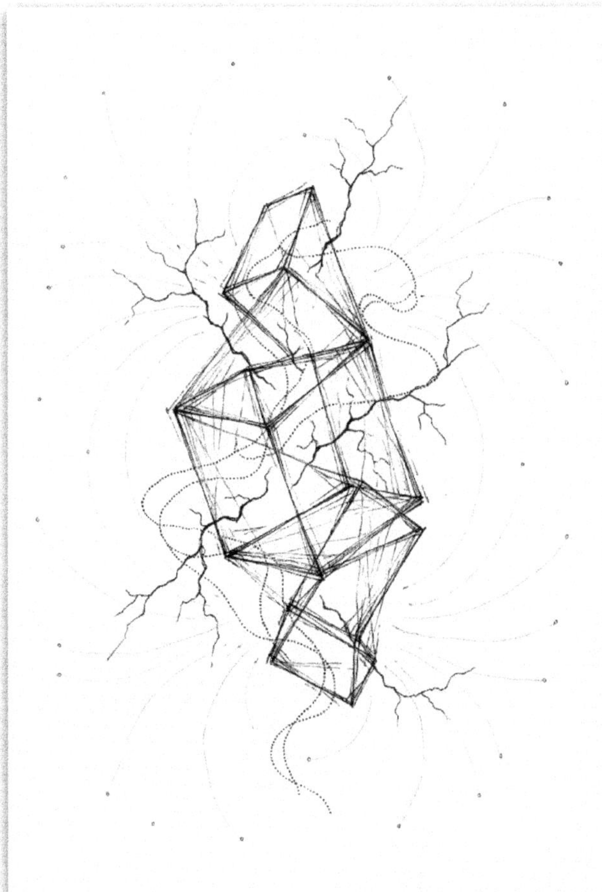

*I watch the mind reach for a label. The label arrives, and the world snaps into objects. The snapping is fast enough to feel like reality.*

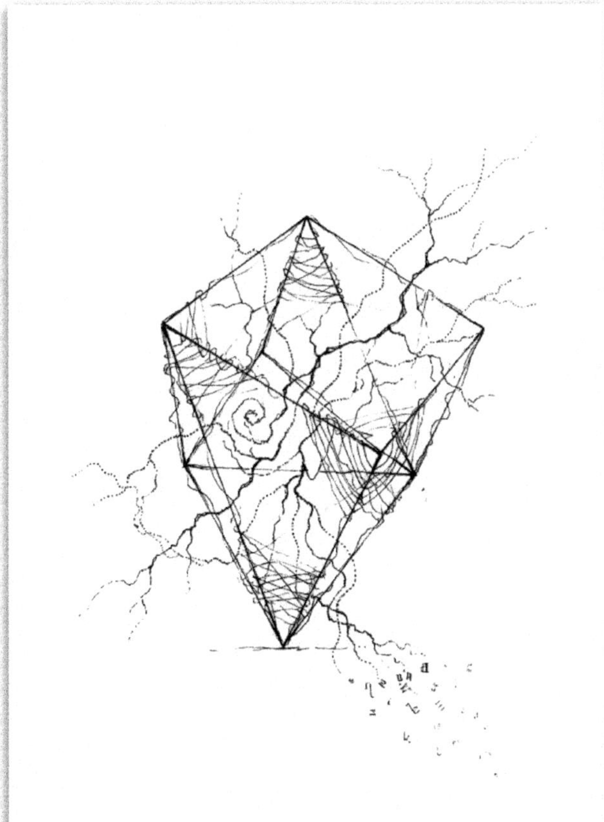

*I can sense how something could be right there and still not appear. Seeing feels conditional—less like possession, more like permission that comes and goes.*

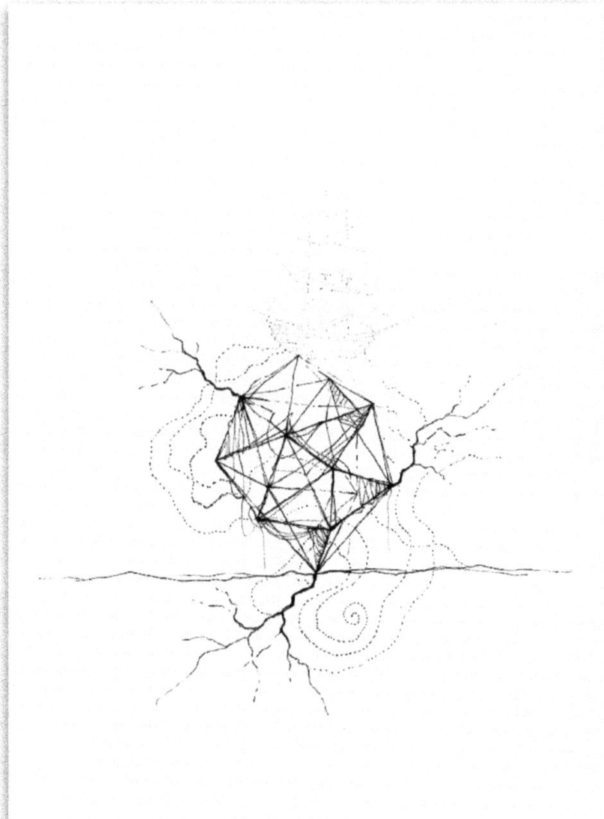

*My attention keeps catching on danger-shapes. It's as if the mind has too many hooks, grabbing at half-signals before the room has time to be ordinary.*

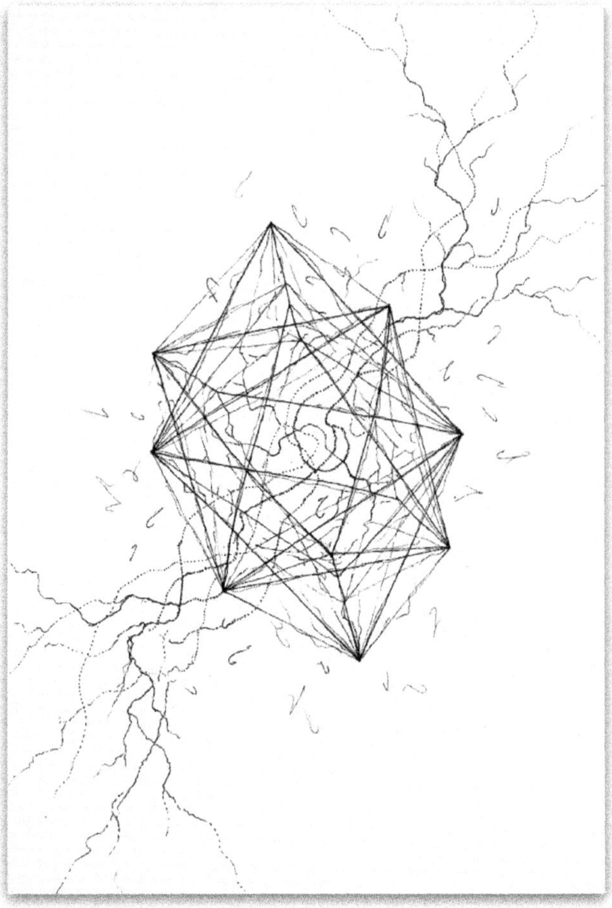

*I ask what I'm thinking, and there is a pause where nothing forms. Not emptiness as an idea—just absence, briefly unshaped.*

*I feel how "me" is assembled—parts gathering into a unity that feels obvious while it's happening. Convincing, and still made.*

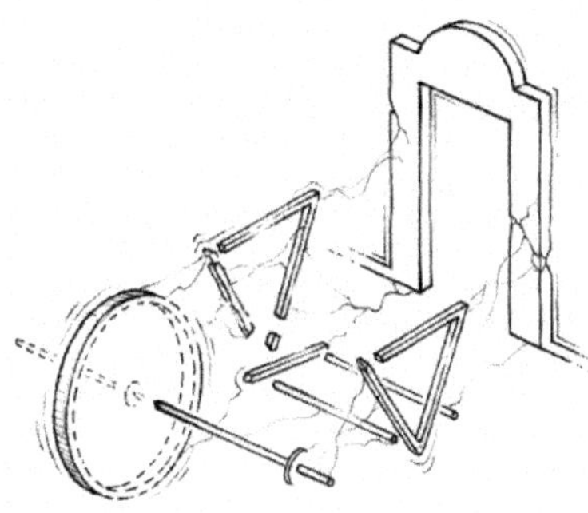

*Layers arrive so quickly they pretend to be one. Body. Sensation. Recognition. Reaction. Awareness. Stacked in an instant, then named as a single "moment."*

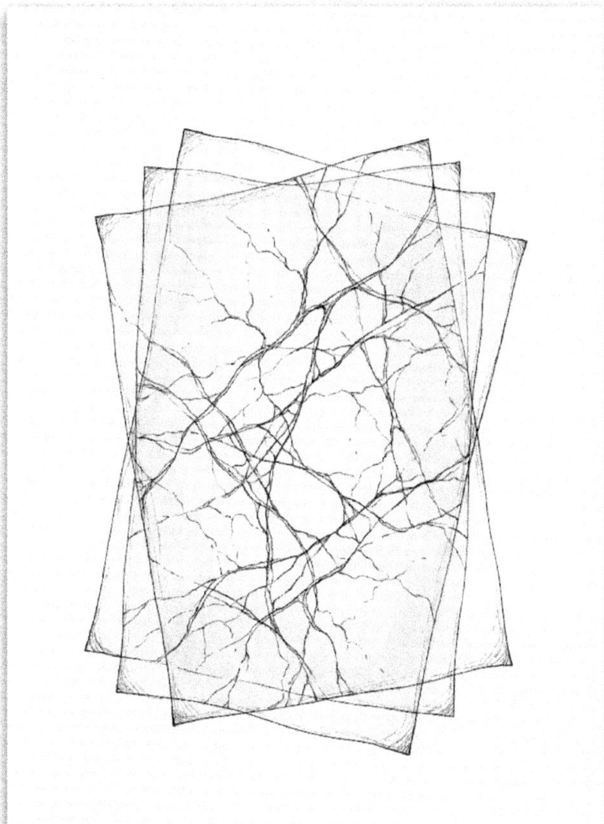

*What I look for is what I find. The search shapes the world before I arrive in it, and then I call the shaping "truth."*

*Behind the small noisy stream, there is a sense of something wider—more like a reservoir than an answer. I can't think it. I can only feel the edge of it.*

*Language feels clumsy here. Straight statements won't hold it. Images do not explain, but they let the feeling remain without collapsing into a verdict.*

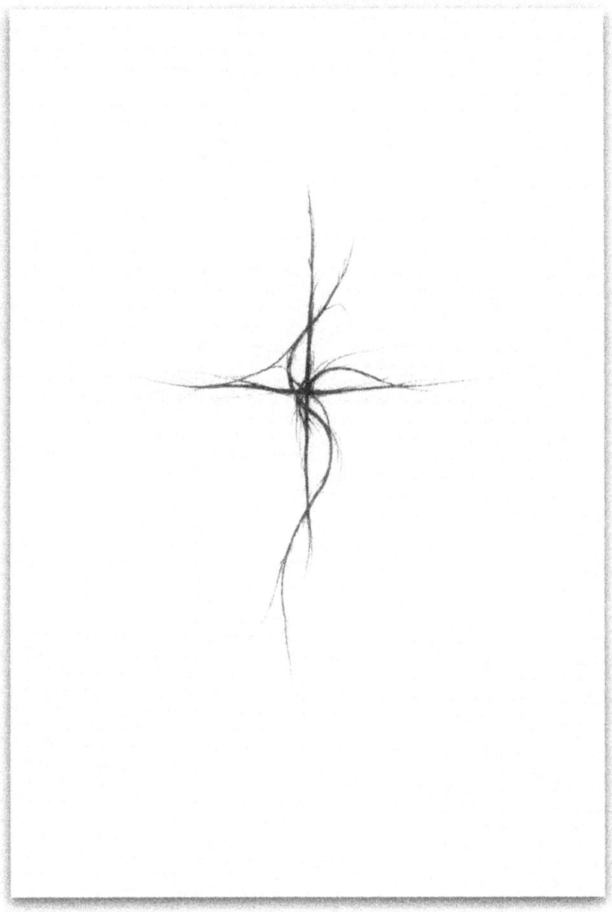

*I sit with the paradox and do not solve it. The need to win the riddle loosens. What remains is a long, patient pondering—unfinished, but quieter.*

# Chapter 10

*I remember the moment the professional mask stopped holding. Something I relied on for "who I am" went quiet. The room didn't change, but my footing did.*

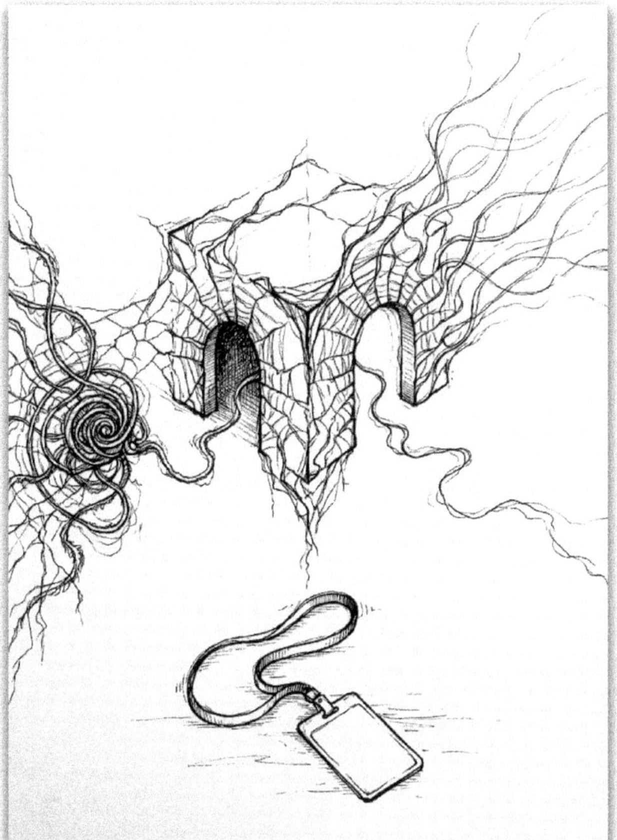

*A restless dissatisfaction grew under the usual answers. I began looking elsewhere, almost reluctantly, as if reaching for something I'd mocked too easily.*

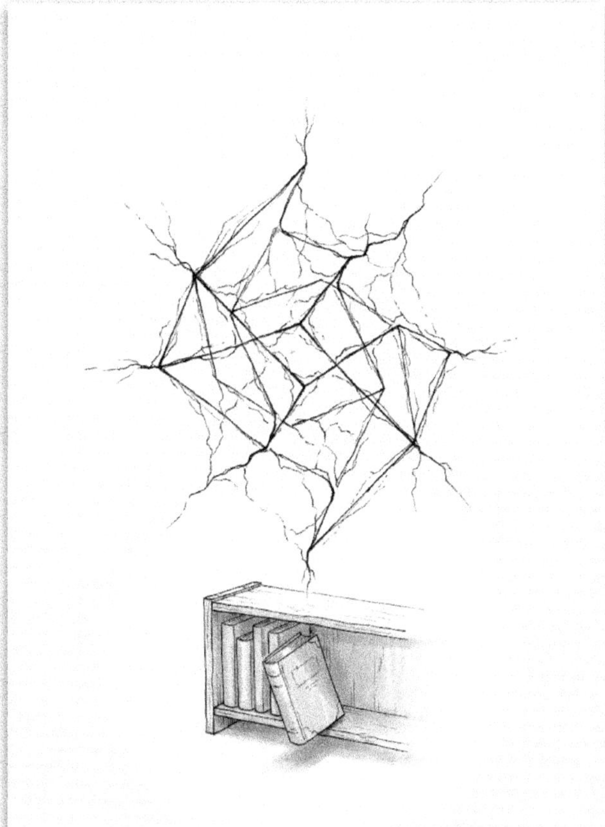

*I notice how quickly I reject what I can't translate. The rejection comes first as a tightening, then as a judgement. It feels like self-protection dressed as certainty.*

*The arguments in my head feel like competing stations. The volume rises; clarity doesn't. I can hear the heat of it, even when I don't choose sides.*

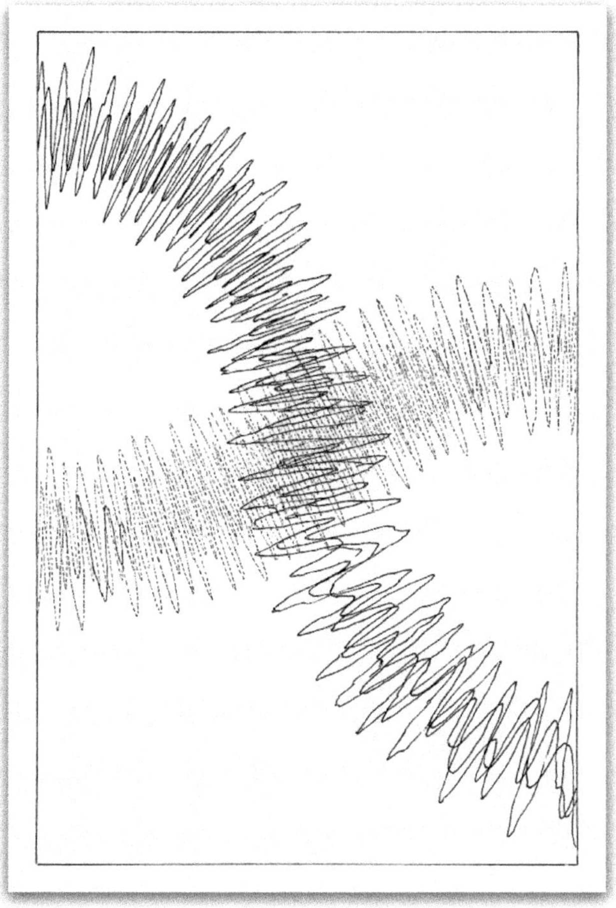

*I hold the pair of opposites and feel the mind stutter. Logic turns back on itself, and for a moment I can't find where to stand.*

*I search for where my mind is and can't place it. It feels present, then it slips—like trying to hold a shape made of weather.*

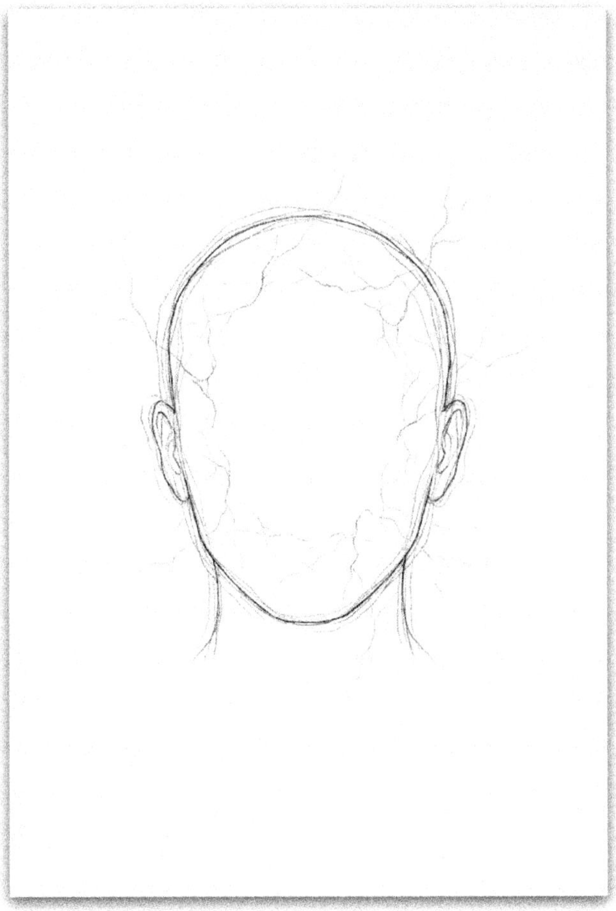

*I glimpse how narrow my focus is. Beyond what I select, something larger seems to hold everything without choosing, without comment.*

*The word "death" appears and my body tightens. Still, another part of me leans in to look—not to solve it, just to admit it is here.*

*I see photographs, feel the stiffening body, hear the older voice—and yet the one noticing feels oddly unchanged. The contrast doesn't prove anything. It only repeats.*

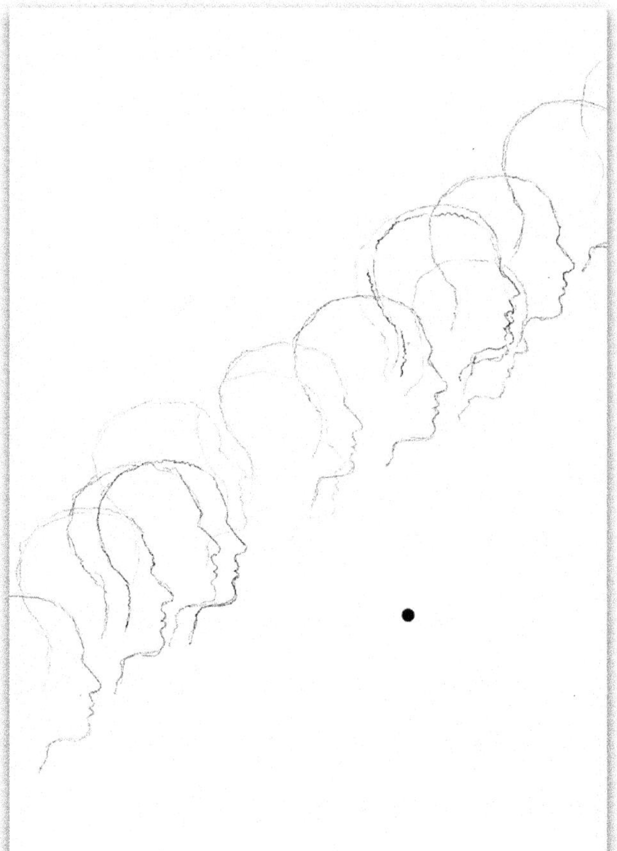

*I let the story arrive without signing my name to it. I hold it lightly, like a tale told at dusk—something that can be listened to without becoming law.*

*I picture a whiteness that isn't a place—more a dissolving. The edges of "me" feel optional for a moment, then return. Nothing is concluded.*

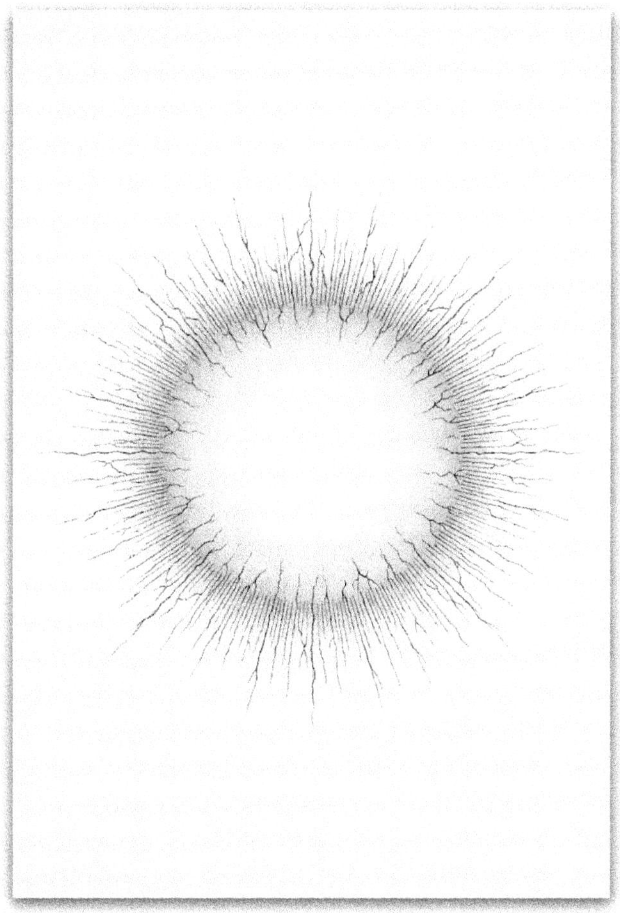

*I imagine time loosening into an interval that can't be counted cleanly. Consciousness dims, then reforms in unfamiliar shapes, and I can't tell what is memory and what is story.*

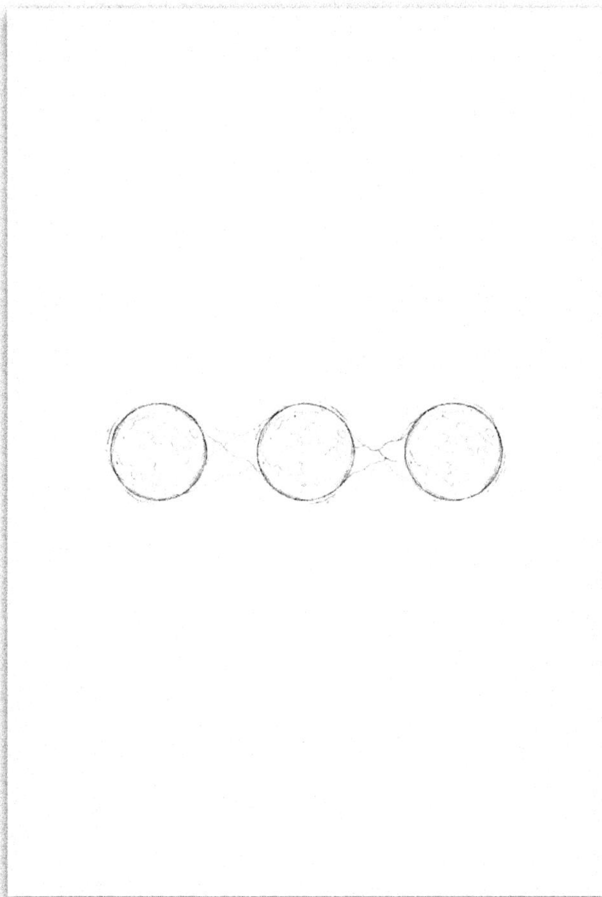

*Figures appear in the mind like options: shelter offered, fear offered. They feel persuasive in opposite directions. I don't know what I'd choose, and I don't have to decide here.*

*I feel the relief of having a sketch, even if it's imperfect. The unknown remains. It is simply less formless than it was a moment ago.*

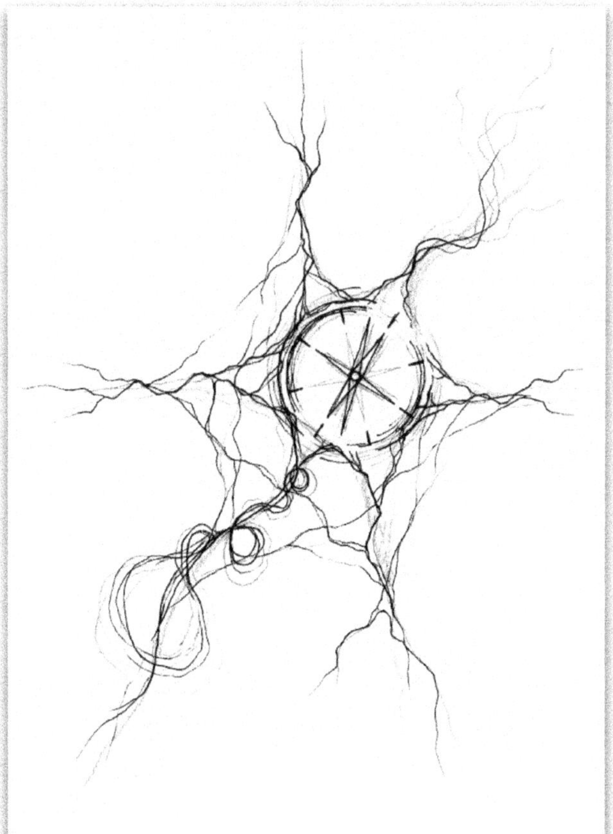

# Chapter 11

*I notice the tone shift into a quiet check-in. Something in me registers the simple fact of continuing.* Not *victory—just the strange dignity of not stopping.*

*I remember how easily the body learns danger. Sometimes it begins early; sometimes it arrives all at once. Either way, the learning feels immediate, as if the nerves keep the score.*

*I recognise the ways I've tried to get away from my own symptoms. The methods don't feel noble or shameful in the moment—just familiar routes the mind already knows.*

*The word impersonal lands with a double edge. Part of me resists its chill. Part of me relaxes, as if some burden of being watched could set itself down.*

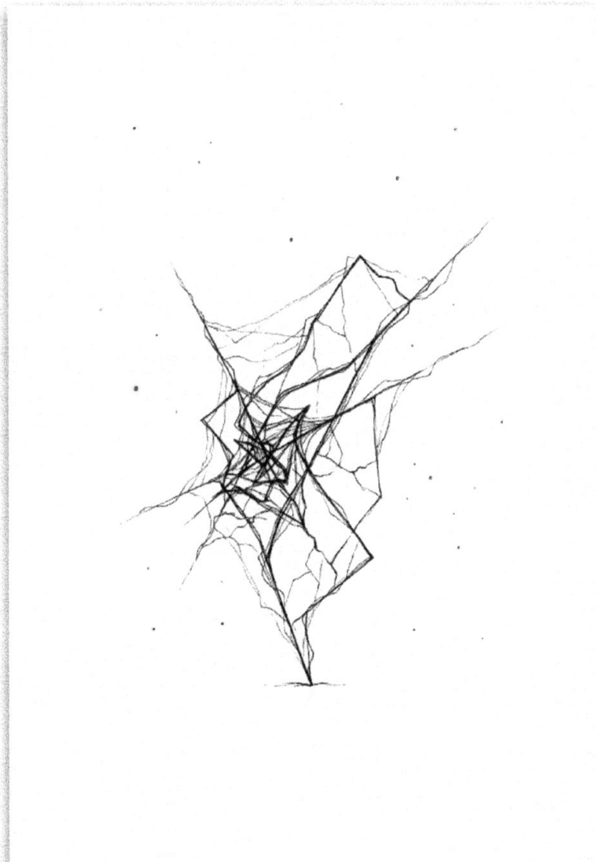

*I picture seals breaking and figures that don't feel gentle. The images frighten me, and still I keep them at the edge of attention—like a dream I don't want, but can't quite refuse.*

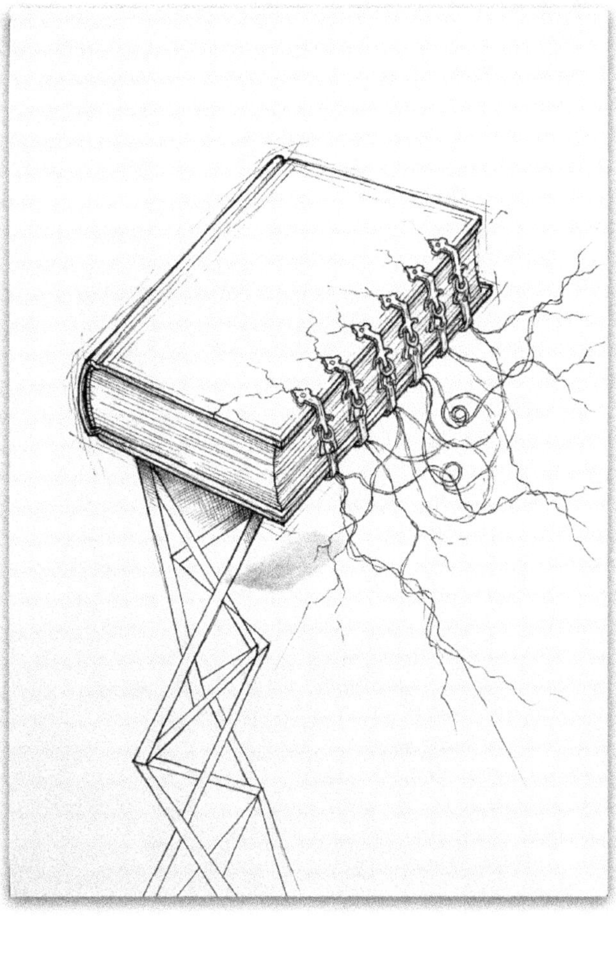

*The idea of stacked inner rooms appears: low to high, each with its own weather. My attention seems to drift up and down the midline without needing a reason.*

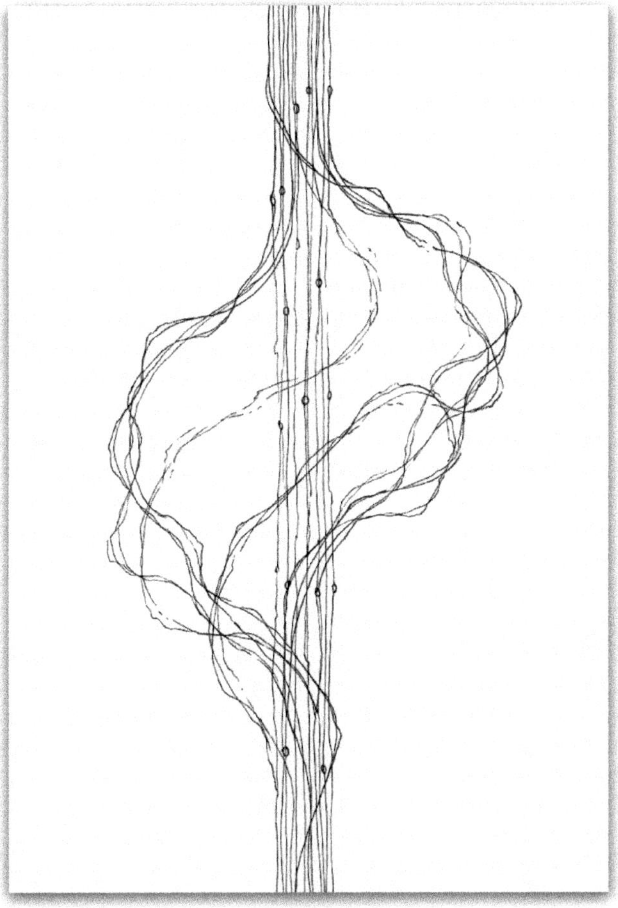

*Fear lives low down—tight, urgent, animal. It doesn't argue. It clenches, and the mind arrives afterwards to justify the clench.*

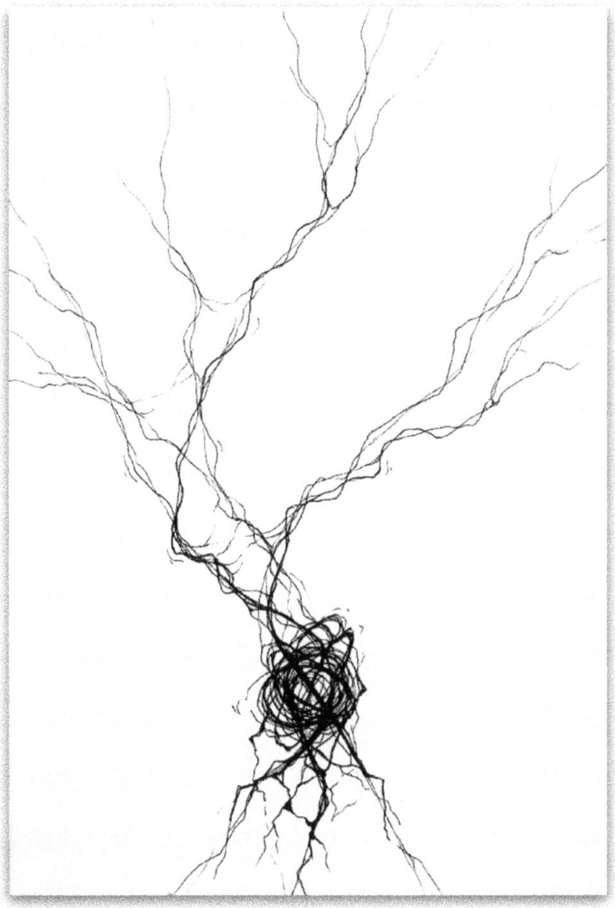

*Shame feels like heat and hiding at once. It arrives with the sense of being measured, even when no one is speaking. The body tries to reduce itself.*

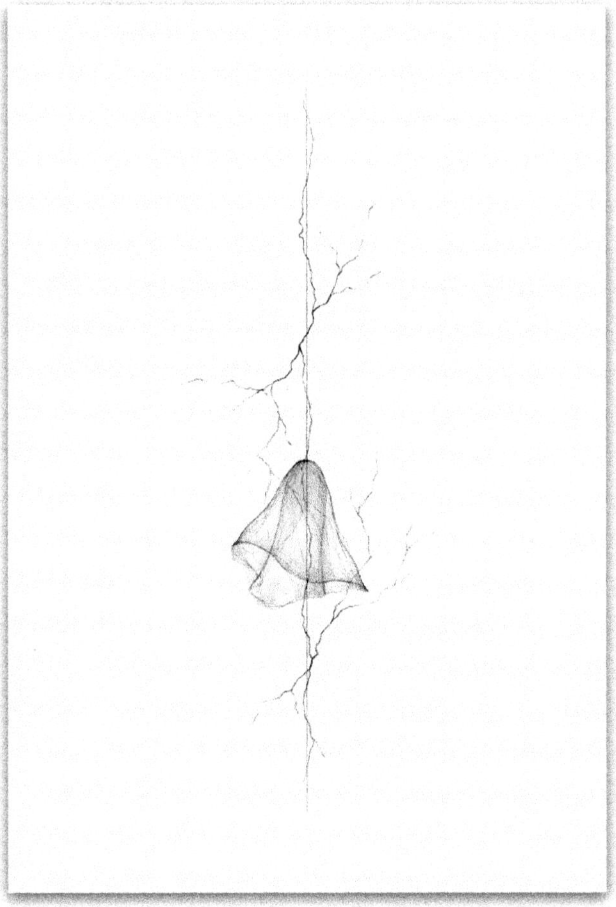

*I recognise desire that doesn't end when it's fed. It keeps asking for "more" even when the body is full, as if the wanting is aimed at something else entirely.*

*Some things feel present without being reachable. Even silence can seem suspicious, as if I'm meant to be worrying, as if vigilance is the default setting.*

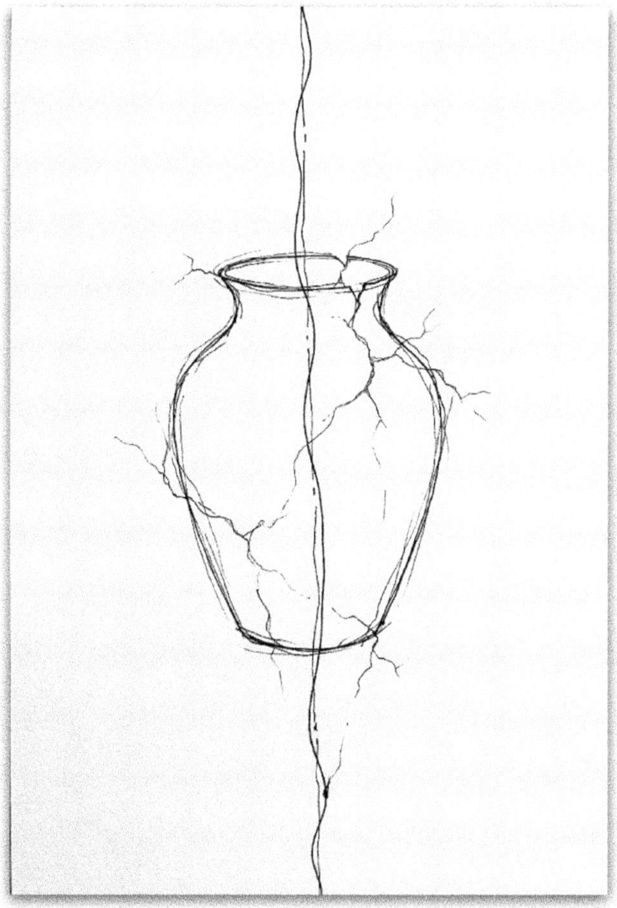

*The language turns toward forgiveness. The inner animal is named—not to be killed, not to be crowned, just acknowledged as something powerful that can carry me if I don't provoke it into panic.*

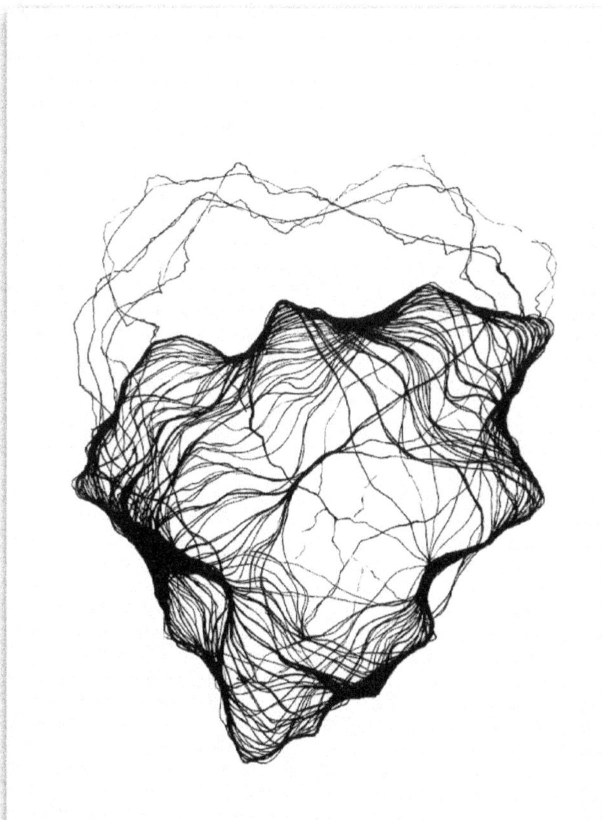

*I picture blame being placed onto something that can carry it. The relief feels real, even while I know the story is symbolic—an old way of moving weight from hand to hand.*

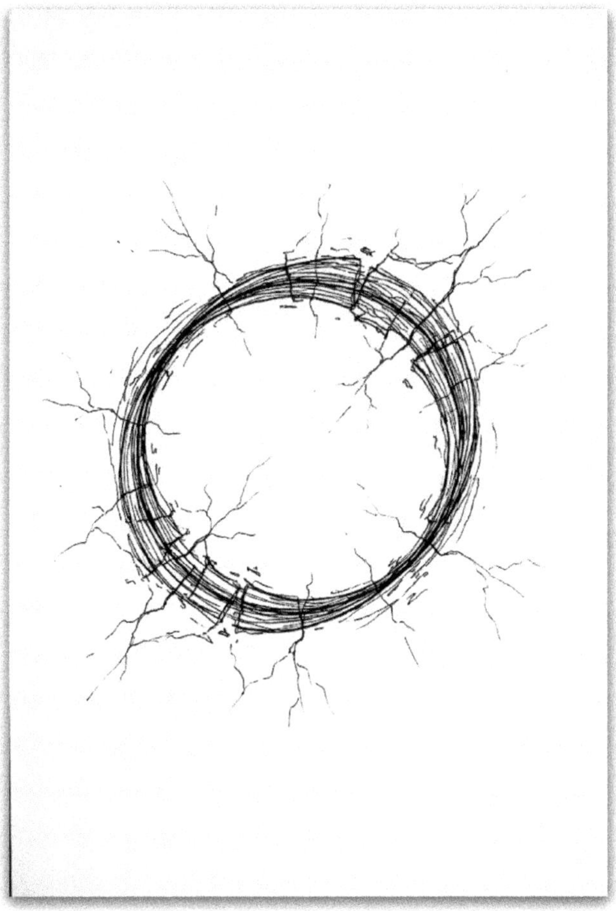

*I recognise the pain of acting against what I know. The judge and the accused feel uncomfortably close —two angles inside the same room, neither fully trustworthy.*

*I end with the image of staying upright while something strong moves underneath. Fear, shame, desire—still possible, still bodily, but less sovereign than they were a moment ago.*

# Chapter 12

*I feel the tone shift into something like farewell, but without finality. There is relief in having arrived, and a faint reluctance to let go of the shared movement that brought me here.*

*A diagram is offered as if it were a compass. I don't understand it yet. Still, it gives the mind something to rest on without gripping too tightly.*

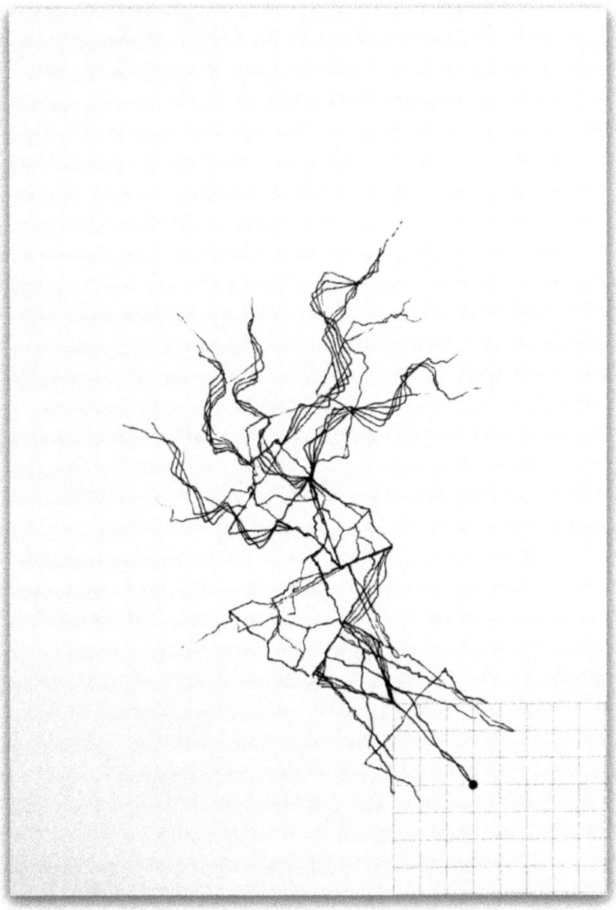

*The word mystical lands, and I notice my body react. Part of me leans in with curiosity. Part of me braces, waiting to be misled. Both responses feel honest.*

*I remember living closer to dreaming, when time felt thin and permeable. I also feel how heavy material thinking became later, as if something subtle was set aside for safety.*

*The body feels like both anchor and threat. I sense its steadiness, and at the same time the familiar shadow of decay that arrives uninvited.*

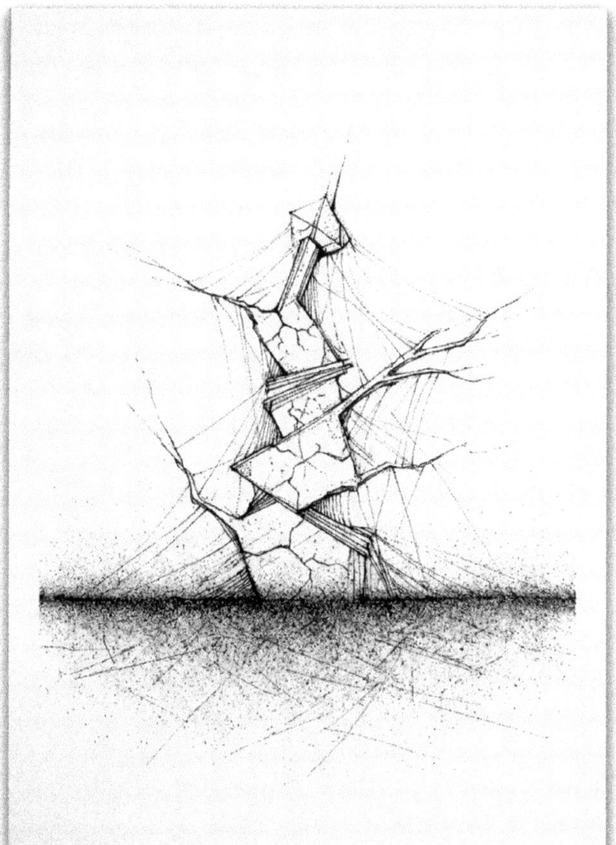

*I picture a sudden knowing of myself—too bright, too defining. With it comes the feeling of being outside something that was once seamless.*

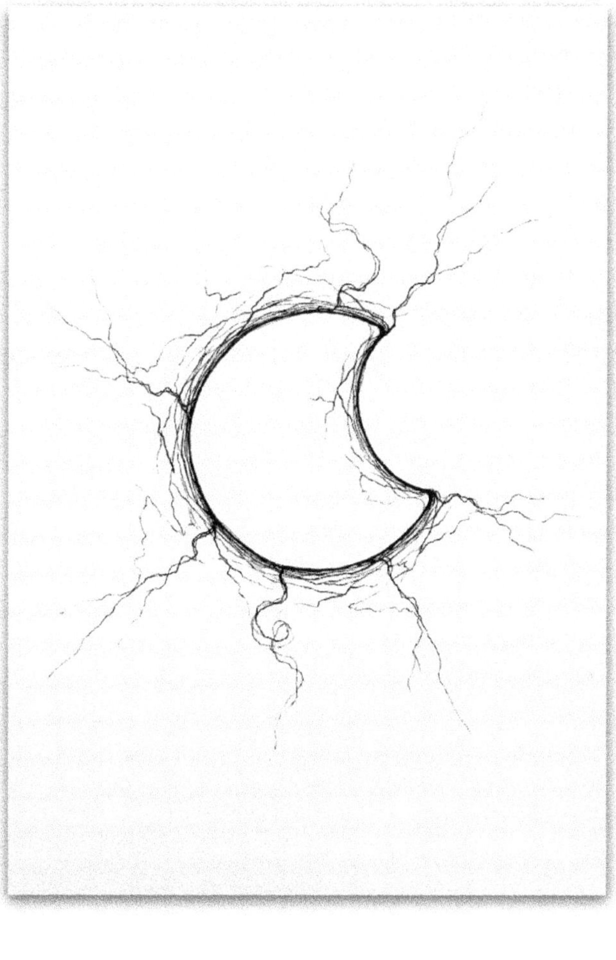

*I can't decide whether the serpent is enemy or teacher. There is the uneasy sense that the wound itself becomes the reason for seeking repair.*

*I sense two strong tendencies inside me: hard division and soft allowance. Between them, a narrow middle line appears—real, but easily missed.*

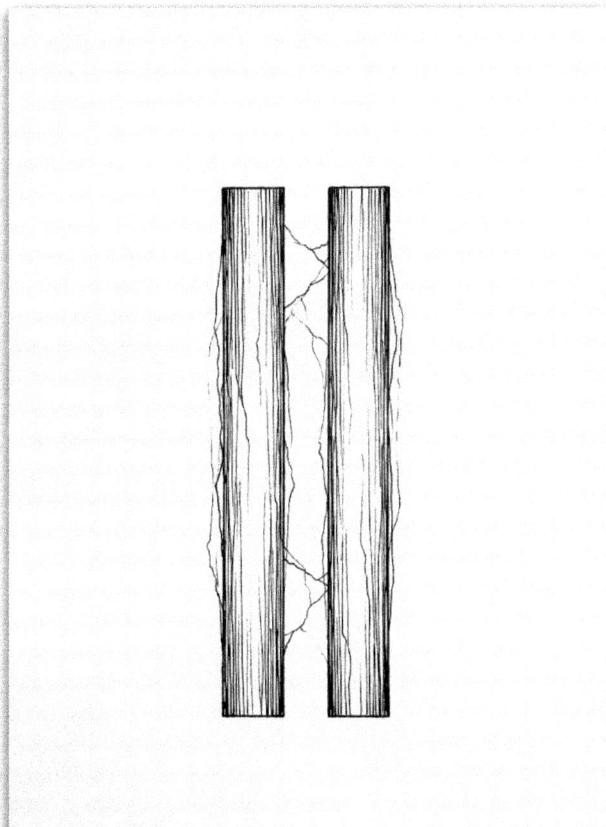

*I recognise a cold safety in thinking too much. It protects, but it isolates, like sleeping inside armour that never quite comes off.*

*What is denied returns wearing a disguise. The figures feel external at first, until I notice they carry my own outline.*

*A voice admits its own starkness and uncertainty. The honesty lands more firmly than any claim of arrival.*

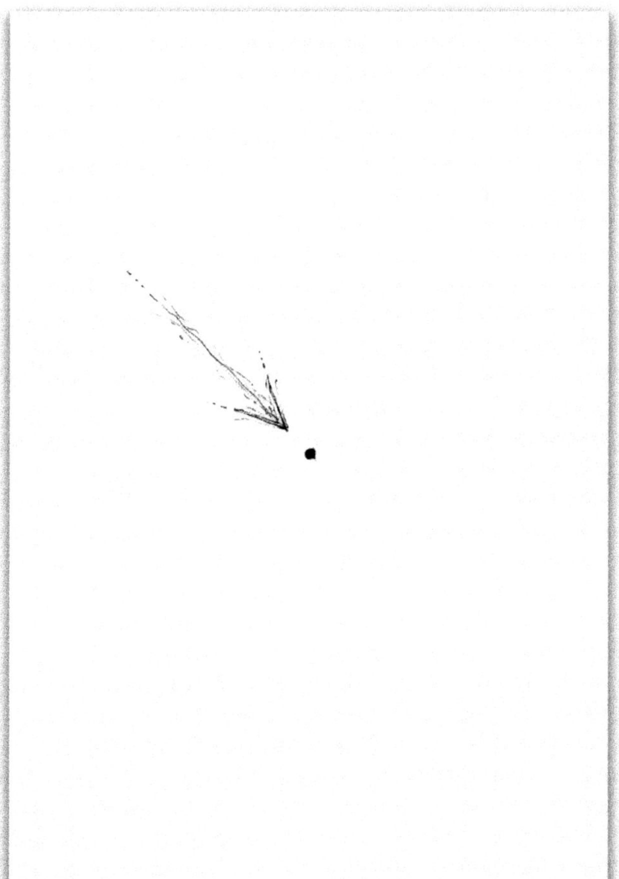

*I imagine stacked atmospheres of mind—material, formed, created, archetypal. The words thin into a feeling of height rather than explanation.*

*When the heart returns to the centre, something softens. Defences loosen without dissolving, and the world feels closer without becoming unreal.*

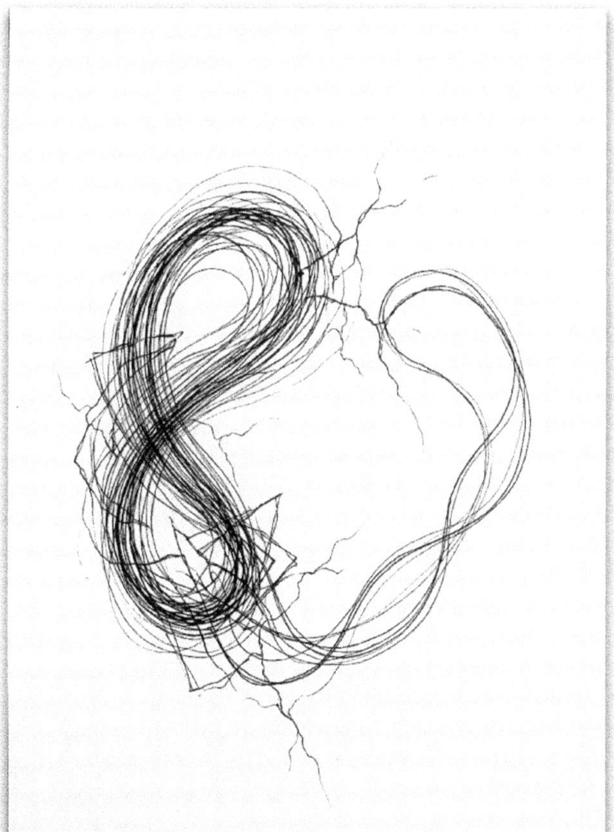

*I end with the sense of something growing quietly upward. Not a finish—more like remembering a direction that was never lost.*

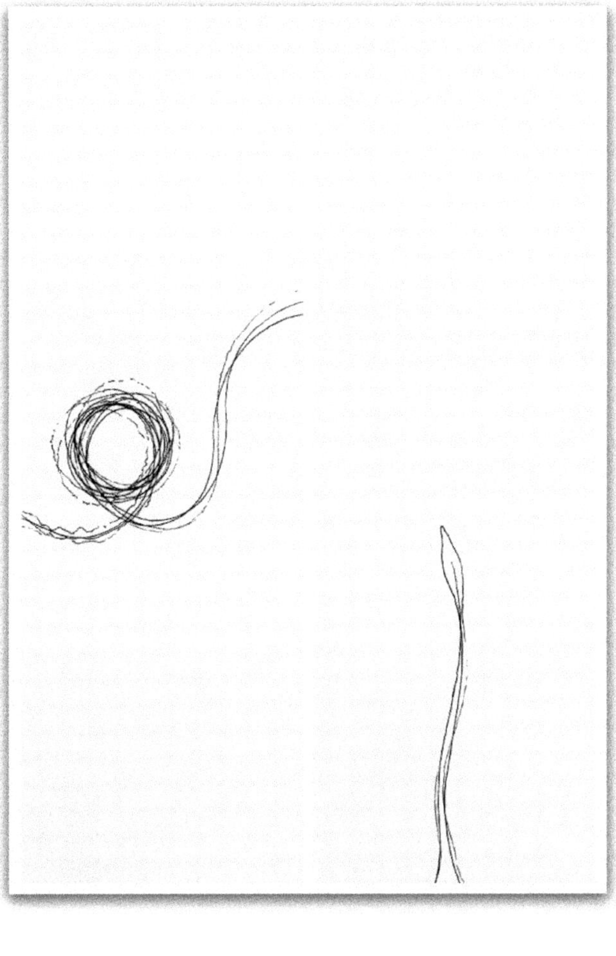

www.ingramcontent.com/pod-product-compliance
Lightning Source LLC
LaVergne TN
LVHW052112210926
848482LV00025B/552
* 9 7 8 1 0 6 8 4 3 1 0 9 8 *